# International
# Airport

# International Airport

## Gaynor Cauter

CONSULTANT: D. P. DAVIES
Chief Test Pilot for Airworthiness Certification
Civil Aviation Authority (UK)

octopus

Designed and created by
Berkeley Publishers Ltd
9 Warwick Court
London WC1

Designed by Keith Worthington
Artwork by Arka Graphics

**First published 1980 by
Octopus Books Limited
59 Grosvenor Street
London W1**

© 1980 Octopus Books Limited

D. L. TO-519-80

ISBN 0 7064 1295 8

Printed in Spain by
Artes Graficas Toledo, S.A.

The author wishes to express particular thanks to
D. P. Davies and to British Airways for their
generous help and cooperation in the preparation
of this book and to the following for their valuable
assistance:

Abex Jetway; Aer Lingus; Aeroflot; Aeroporti di
Roma; Aeroports de Paris; Air Canada;
Air France; Air-India; Air Service Training; Airbus
Industrie; Airline Publications and Sales Ltd;
Airwork Services Ltd; Alitalia; Angus Fire Armour
Ltd; Boeing Commercial Airplane Company;
Braniff International; Britax (PMG) Ltd; British
Aerospace; British Airports Authority; British
Caledonian Airways; CESCA; Central Office of
Information (UK); Chamberlain Managing Group;
Chubb Fire Security; City of Chicago (Dept of
Aviation); Civil Aviation Authority (UK); Dallas-Fort
Worth Airport; Dan-Air Services Ltd; Decca
Navigator Co. Ltd; M. W. Edghill Equipment Ltd;
Ferranti Ltd; the Editor and staff of Flight
International; General Electric Aircraft Engine
Group; Hallam Engineering; Herman Smith Ltd;
Houchin Ltd; Interflug; Jeppesen and Co.; KLM
Royal Dutch Airlines; Lockheed-California Co.;
LOT Polish Airlines; Marconi Avionics Ltd;
McDonnell Douglas Corporation; Miles Dufon
Ltd; National Airlines; National Air Traffic
Services; Power Lifts; Qantas Airways; Redifon
Ltd; RFD Inflatables Ltd; Rockwell-Collins
International Inc.; Rolls-Royce Ltd (Aero Division);
L. A. Rumbold Ltd (BSG International); Singapore
Airlines; Smiths Industries; Sperry Gyroscope;
Sunderstrand Advanced Technology Group;
Thomson-CSF; Trans Com (Sunderstrand Data
Control Inc.); Trans World Airlines; Trepel AG;
United Airlines; Wardair Canada; Weston
Instruments.

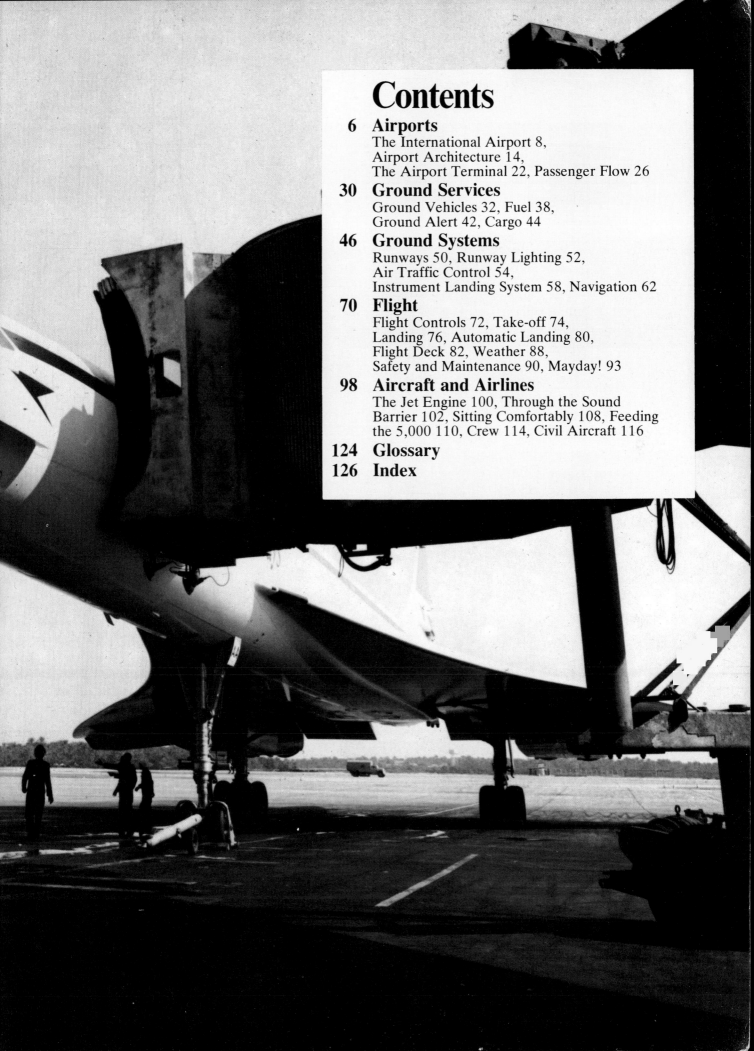

# Contents

**6 Airports**
The International Airport 8,
Airport Architecture 14,
The Airport Terminal 22, Passenger Flow 26

**30 Ground Services**
Ground Vehicles 32, Fuel 38,
Ground Alert 42, Cargo 44

**46 Ground Systems**
Runways 50, Runway Lighting 52,
Air Traffic Control 54,
Instrument Landing System 58, Navigation 62

**70 Flight**
Flight Controls 72, Take-off 74,
Landing 76, Automatic Landing 80,
Flight Deck 82, Weather 88,
Safety and Maintenance 90, Mayday! 93

**98 Aircraft and Airlines**
The Jet Engine 100, Through the Sound
Barrier 102, Sitting Comfortably 108, Feeding
the 5,000 110, Crew 114, Civil Aircraft 116

**124 Glossary**
**126 Index**

*An Air-India 707 sits amid a variety of wide-bodied contemporaries at London Heathrow, including a Venezuelan DC-10, two British Airways TriStars and five 747s.*

# Airports

# The International Airport

If the experts are right, the total volume of passengers flying by air will increase to 945,000,000 per annum by 1988, more than half of them passing through the United States, travelling some 1,323,000,000,000 km (822,000,000,000 miles). This is roughly the same as flying one passenger 33 million times around the world! Few of these passengers stepping off an aircraft are aware of how many people have been involved in making their journey safe and comfortable. An airport is a self-contained community with a vast infrastructure of personnel, vehicles and equipment working round the clock to keep the whole mechanism running smoothly and efficiently. But although an airport is self-contained so far as its facilities are concerned, it can never operate in isolation from the community in which it is situated. Some localities

are more tolerant than others to the undoubted disadvantages of living in close proximity to an international airport. Few make mention of the benefits in terms of trade and employment.

## From grass fields...

Many airports have grown up from primitive grass fields and have gradually encroached on the surrounding area as extra space has become necessary. Others have been built from scratch and, where possible, the more far-sighted designers have allowed space for expansion. Dallas-Fort Worth in Texas is a good example of forward planning on a grand scale. Developers

there have set aside no less than 73 km² (28 square miles) to accommodate expansion. But whichever way an airport evolves there are bound to be protests and opposition, which in recent years have reached almost terrorist proportions. Narita, Japan's latest airport, has probably suffered most at the hands of determined protesters, with passengers being searched and heavy security not only in the airport terminal but around the perimeter as well. It would seem that everyone wants to be able to walk straight into an airport, climb aboard an aircraft and take off for their destination without delay – but few want the facilities on their doorstep.

Noise and pollution have always been the main problems. At some airports there is also the danger of aircraft crashing into a built-up area and endangering the lives of local residents. Usually the

site for an airport is chosen with this in mind but in a tiny area such as Hong Kong there is little choice. A pilot approaching the runway has to keep his wits about him and hope that he will not lose his undercarriage on a hotel roof some 15 m (50 ft) below. This problem of space is hard to overcome but the problems of noise and pollution are being dealt with successfully. The new generation of jet engines is much quieter and wide-bodied aircraft are so much larger that the number of landings and take-offs is considerably reduced. Stricter noise controls over urban areas have encouraged, if not forced, the development of more 'sociable' aircraft. Radar and navigation systems have become more sophisticated, making flying safer, and improved building techniques have made runways sturdier and more capable of bearing the load of large capacity aircraft without requiring any more space to accommodate them.

While an airport has to work side by side with the surrounding community, it also has to cater for its own army of staff and personnel. It must cope with the constant flow of passengers and crew it was built to serve. The more efficiently it is run the more profitable it will be as satisfied customers, both public and airlines, are more likely to make use of it.

In addition to the obvious essentials such as terminals, runways, taxiways and control tower, there are vast expanses of airport never visited by the passengers. These are just as vital to the running of the whole. There must be large warehousing facilities for freight, parking for private and commercial aircraft not in use at that moment, parking and maintenance areas for the fleets of ground vehicles, maintenance hangars for the aircraft and accommodation for operations staff and crew. There are health-inspectors, immigration officials, customs officers, airline employees, maintenance crews, cargo and baggage handlers, catering staff, drivers, security officials and airline personnel, to mention but a few.

Ideally, an airport should be easily accessible by road, rail and, more recently, by helicopter. Airports in London, for example, have helicopter 'links' to ferry people from airport to airport or to the centre of the city. There must be long-term car parks for passengers who use their own transport, and with 30,000,000 or more passengers passing through in one year even a small percentage with cars necessitates an enormous amount of parking space at any one time.

## Biggest and busiest

Although London Heathrow now has the largest flow of international traffic, Chicago O'Hare is the world's busiest airport, with a huge flow of internal as well as international flights. More than 40,000,000 passengers pass through the airport every year and at present Chicago holds the record for aircraft movements at 777,000 in one year with a flow of 50,000,000 passengers.

These figures sound impressive and compared with those of even ten years ago they are, but they have by no means reached their peak. The International Civil Aviation Organization (ICAO) has estimated that the next ten years will see the largest period of growth in the history of civil air transport. The estimated cost of this growth is £230 billion. The largest area of expansion is in the Third World countries, where industrial development and expanding economies are demanding more facilities for communication with other countries. Nigeria has no fewer than 12 projects in hand, at a cost of more than £6¼ billion, while Zaire has 30 smaller projects on the drawing board and Egypt 4. If the statistics can be believed there will be no shortage of customers for any of these airports or for the already-established ones.

## Twenty-five million gallons of fuel

All this flying requires fuel — millions of gallons of it. A Boeing 747 can happily swallow about 200,000 litres (44,000 gal) at a time. With a dozen or more in need of refuelling every day, in addition to all the other aircraft passing through, there must be storage facilities for vast quantities of fuel. New York's John F. Kennedy airport has tackled this problem by installing a special fuel farm which will hold up to 114,000,000 litres (25,000,000 gal).

*Amsterdam's busy Schiphol Airport, one of Europe's busiest passenger terminals.*

A view of the tower and part of the terminal at Dubai International. Built by Costain International Limited in 1971, Dubai is one of several fine-looking new airports built in the United Arab Emirates. Vast expanses of unclaimed land and ample financial resources have made the UAE airport authorities the envy of many nations. Even where the money is available to build an airport which will fulfil its purpose in years to come, it is often hard to find sufficient land space without encroaching on urban developments or upsetting local ecologists. Since it was built, Dubai has already been extended by the construction of a second runway and a new terminal to anticipate an increase in traffic should the present growth rate continue into the 1980s.

# Minimum standards

All major airports have their own emergency services, some more efficient than others. There is a minimum standard set by ICAO below which an airport cannot obtain a licence to operate. Chances are never taken, and if there is even the slightest possibility of trouble emergency services will turn out at once and be ready on the taxiways for an incoming aircraft. A 747 approaching Heathrow recently reported smoke coming from one of the engines as the aircraft was about 3 km (2 miles) from touchdown. Within seconds the firefighting vehicles were racing to the far end of the runway and a few minutes later back-up support was arriving from the local fire brigades in the neighbourhood. Luckily it turned out to be a false alarm and they were not needed – but no one took any chances with more than 300 passengers and crew on board.

Medical services often present more of a problem. While a fleet of heavy-duty firefighting vehicles might be able to put out a blazing aircraft, a vast fleet of ambulances and an equally large number of hospital beds would be required to accommodate the injured. There has been severe criticism of various airports for being under-equipped but, as one observer ruefully pointed out, the chances of there being 300 passengers still alive to take to hospital would not be very great if a jet aircraft were to crash.

# The safest way

Despite this sobering thought, flying is still considered to be the safest way to travel – some 25 times safer than travelling by road. Once the initial fear has passed, most people are eager to board an aircraft and to sample the airline's hospitality. Non-stop flights of 17 hours at a time have put the airlines' initiative and imagination to the test. There is great competition among them as to who can make their passengers most comfortable, serve them the best food and free drinks and keep them entertained throughout the flight. More people can afford to fly than ever before and prices are becoming more competitive all the time. In fact, it looks as if the international airport will be doing good business for a long time to come.

*The vast expanse of Dallas-Fort Worth International Airport in Texas.*

# Airport Architecture

Unlike a railway station, an airport is not merely a terminal for travellers. It is a symbol of national prestige. Millions are spent on building terminals which are not only functional but which look spectacular as well. Some of the world's leading architects have created superb 'flights of fancy' at enormous cost to accommodate the airlines and their passengers. The real test of the design is not just how impressive it looks but how well it actually works – and work it must if it is to handle 4,000,000 passengers a year.

The ideal design for an airport terminal should combine clean, uncluttered lines which will be slow to date, creating a focal point within an airport without being obtrusive or interferring with the

Below *Dubai is yet another fine example of the beautiful airports being built in the UAE.*
Right *Interior of Sharjah.*

aircraft movements and the traffic control. A great tower block of glass with the sun shining on it a short distance from the control tower is hardly the ideal construction when there are low flying aircraft in the vicinity. Alternatively, a huge, sprawling complex of long corridors and vast open spaces may take up far too much valuable ground space and require a great deal of leg work on the part of the passengers.

Ideally the terminal building must be able to accommodate passengers, airline check-ins, customs and all the other necessary facilities such as restaurants and shops comfortably, without wasting space yet without crowding either. It is quite a demanding task to design such a building and different architects have approached the problem in very different ways according to the situation of the airport and the requirements of the airlines and authorities. The results have been, for the most part, refreshing to say the least.

## Superb Saarinen

Awards have been won for the design of airport terminals. Eero Saarinen won such an award for his design for the TWA terminal at John F. Kennedy. The whole building echoes the theme of flight. Two lateral vaults soar up into great glass and concrete cantilevers like huge wings. The design is graceful and daring yet very unlikely to date. Inside, the impression is of a cool, vaulted shell full of space and light. This is an important feature of any terminal from the passenger's point of view, particularly for nervous fliers and tired business executives. No one wants to be bustled and crowded in a thronging mass of fellow travellers while announcements ring in their ears and baggage trolleys threaten their feet and ankles. There must be comfortable seating arrangements, easily read flight departure dis-

plays and audible but unobtrusive announcements.

The choice of materials and furnishings makes a great difference to the overall impression. Marble, tiles, glass and smooth rendered concrete give a feeling of space and calm. Plants make a great difference by softening harsh lines and adding a touch of colour. There is no place for fussy and complicated details. Every feature of the building must be functional, serving the passengers in the most efficient way possible.

Saarinen's genius for design can be seen at another airport in the United States. Dulles International features a long glass and concrete terminal which sweeps up and lunges forward towards the approaching passengers like a great hammock. Radical new passenger movement facilities were incorporated in the design for Dulles, including mobile lounges to ferry the passengers in comfort from the terminal to the aircraft. The whole airport is a masterpiece of design. Covering 40 km² (15½ square miles) it lies some 40 km (25 miles) west of Washington DC, served by a special highway for easy access. The control tower at Dulles is particularly distinctive with its pagoda-style control room perched on a sheer white stem, topped by a large white ball. It is one of the tallest control towers in the world and for good reason, considering the size of the airfield and position of the runways.

There are three runways in use at Dulles, two at 3,500 m (11,500 ft) and one shorter one at 3,000 m (10,000 ft). The two longer runways lie parallel at extreme sides of the airfield, with the terminal area positioned at right angles in the centre. Unlike London Heathrow, where the third runway cuts across the other two, the third runway at Dulles lies at an angle, away from the far end of one of the longer runways. This arrangement allows for the third runway to be used without halting all other incoming and outgoing traffic.

## Room for expansion

Dulles may be large in area and close to the capital city but it is by no means the largest or the busiest airport in the United States. In terms of actual geographical size, the largest must be Dallas-Fort Worth. There had been an airfield near Forth Worth since before the Second World War but the present airport is a new development. It is unique in its entire design concept in that it is one of the few airports that has been planned with the long-term future not merely in mind, but actually catered for.

An area of 73 km² (28 square miles) has been set aside to accommodate expansion as and when it becomes necessary. It embodies good looks with the latest thinking in facilities for both passengers and aircraft.

At present Dallas has three runways and four terminals, although allowance has been made for three times this number, both of runways and terminals, should they be required in the future. The two parallel runways allow for uninterrupted aircraft movement both in and out while a shorter, cross-wind runway lies at right angles to the other two. The terminals are semi-circular in shape, the outside edge of each providing maximum space for aircraft to park. This reduces the distance passengers have to walk. Dallas serves over 17,000,000 international and domestic passengers a year and it has room to accommodate as many more as care to fly there. It is the home base of Braniff, one of America's major international airlines.

Despite the vast scale on which Dallas-Fort Worth has been planned it is by no means the busiest airport in the United States. Here the claim to fame lies firmly with Chicago O'Hare. Chicago not only has the largest number of aircraft movements in America, but in the world if domestic flights are included. It has no fewer than seven runways and handles more than double the number of passengers handled by Dallas in a year. There are three main terminal buildings which are all connected for easy access, with separate restaurants and cocktail lounges housed in a circular building known as the Rotunda. The aircraft park in bays along extensions which fan out in a semi-circle from the main terminal area. Of the seven runways, there are three sets running parallel with a 1,628 m (5,340 ft) one for short take-offs. With over 750,000 aircraft movements a year on seven runways it is easy to appreciate the need for 150 air traffic controllers.

## Gateway to America

New York is served by three main airports, the busiest of which is John F. Kennedy. Generally known as Idlewild until the early 1960s, Kennedy airport is built on reclaimed land by the edge of Jamaica Bay. Its passenger handling rate is only half that of O'Hare but it is the gateway to the East Coast for transatlantic flights. There are nine passenger terminals built on an 'island' surrounded by a ring of aircraft parking bays. Five runways are in use, including a long one, 4,440 m (14,570 ft), and a short one, 844 m (2,760 ft), for light aircraft and business jets. Unlike many airports in Europe, Kennedy has allowed

*Seven satellites surround the main terminal at Charles de Gaulle airport which began operations in 1978.*

individual airlines such as Pan American, Trans World, Lufthansa and Air France to provide their own terminal facilities. The competitive spirit of the commercial airlines has led to the design of some spectacular buildings not least of which is the TWA terminal mentioned earlier.

Leaving John F. Kennedy, the next port of call must be London Heathrow. Architecturally this is not the most stunning of airports. However, Heathrow carries the heaviest load of international air traffic in the world even if its design and facilities are not the most modern. It evolved from a war-time aerodrome about 24 km (15 miles) from central London. The sprawling suburbs of the city surround it on all sides and there is constant antagonism from residents against the aircraft. It is estimated that Heathrow will have reached its capacity of 30,000,000 passengers by 1980 and there is strong pressure to build a fourth terminal to cope with this increase until a third London airport can be built. This may not be for some time as the actual site of this new airport is still far from settled, although Stansted is now thought to be the favourite.

Heathrow suffers from a lack of space. The terminal area is penned in between the two parallel runways which are most often used, and a third, shorter one which cuts across one side of the field. Access has been improved recently by the completion of an underground railway link from the centre of London — albeit a few years late. Passengers have the option of checking in for British Airways flights either at the airport, or in the city and travelling out by bus. The motorway serving the airport is also the main trunk road to the West of England and suffers from severe congestion, particularly during the commuter period. A large part of the road is elevated and is therefore impossible to widen. The fastest way to leave the airport is by helicopter. The 'Link' service now operates, ferrying passengers to Gatwick, London's second airport, for connecting flights.

Whether the third airport will ever materialize to relieve Heathrow and Gatwick is open to conjecture. Airport authorities and local pressure groups seem no closer to finding a mutually acceptable site than they were ten years ago. In the meantime London's second airport at Gatwick is having to manage with only one terminal building

*Above The cool, airy interior of Eero Saarinen's TWA terminal at John F. Kennedy International, New York. Left Frankfurt, one of Europe's largest air cargo ports and also one of the busiest passenger terminals.*

and one runway, which is also very congested. New parking facilities for aircraft are being added but there is little prospect of the second runway, although a second terminal is now being considered.

Travelling south-east, the next airport worthy of mention is Charles de Gaulle, Paris's prestigious new international terminus. It was planned from the very beginning to be an international airport with facilities that could cope with the growth of passenger and aircraft movements. Orly Airport still handles a larger portion of international traffic, but de Gaulle will take over once the facilities are fully developed and operational. The space-age architecture and the sheer scale of the undertaking make a fitting home for the Air France Concordes. The great circular Aerogare incorporates multi-storey car parking as well as all the usual passenger facilities. Aircraft are parked round satellite stations which radiate from the central terminal. Passenger access to the aircraft is through underground tunnels below the tarmac on moving walkways.

At present there is one runway in use at Charles de Gaulle but the planners have taken into account the need for as many as four should they be required. The parallel runways are well spaced out and a very tall control tower, 80 m (263 ft) high, oversees all aircraft movements. The airport is conveniently situated about 15 km (10 miles) from Paris and is now handling nearly 9,000,000 passengers a year.

One of the busiest international airports in Europe for both passengers and freight is Amsterdam Schiphol. The airport is built on reclaimed land just outside Amsterdam itself and lies 4 m (13 ft) below sea level. The modern terminal complex is spacious and well-designed to handle today's wide-bodied aircraft. The entire terminal facility was rebuilt in the 1960s on a separate site from the original buildings, and extra aircraft parking bays have been added to cope with the larger-capacity jets. Space has not been a problem here and the airport is expected to maintain its fitness for purpose for many years to come.

*Timeless architecture for modern technology, Sharjah glistens against the clear desert sky.*

The terminal and control buildings form a long, integrated complex with clean, functional lines without architectural extravagance. Long Y-shaped piers accommodate both passenger and cargo aircraft, of which there are a large number passing through Schiphol. Access to the airport has been improved by the construction of a rail link to Amsterdam and passenger facilities are of the highest standard, including an excellent duty-free shop. There are four runways in use at Schiphol, catering for over 130,000 aircraft movements a year. It is also the home base of KLM Royal Dutch Airlines, the national flag carrier of the Netherlands, which began flights from there in 1920. Schiphol is one of the finest airports in Western Europe and is an impressive example of thoughtful planning and design, incorporating everything including an aviation museum.

Even busier than Schiphol is Frankfurt, West Germany's major airport. Frankfurt Rhein/Main handles nearly twice as many passengers and aircraft movements as Schiphol and is another good example of modern airport design thinking. The whole complex has been rebuilt during the past 20 years, involving one of the largest-scale construction programmes ever undertaken in Germany. The airport buildings are not the most attractive architecturally but they follow clean, functional lines similar to Gatwick and Orly.

Frankfurt is now capable of handling over 30,000,000 passengers a year, which compares favourably with London Heathrow. Its position in the centre of Western Europe makes it an important airport not only for flights terminating in Germany but as a stop-over for long distance flights to and from the Middle and Far East. Lufthansa, Germany's flag carrier, has extensive ground facilities for both passenger and cargo services at Frankfurt. There are two runways in use, handling over 200,000 aircraft movements a year, on the site where the Zeppelins were based before the last war.

During the past 20 years new airports have sprung up all over Europe as the demands of air traffic have increased. Many major cities can no longer cope with just one airport and some, such as London, are finding it hard to cope with two. Rome's answer to relieving the

burden of air traffic is the new Leonardo da Vinci airport, built to replace the previous airport at Ciampino. It is situated on the coast, 30 km (20 miles) south-west of Rome itself. It is an excellent site for an airport with clear, unobstructed airspace all around, on flat country and with plenty of groundspace to accommodate future expansion. There are three runways in use at present handling nearly 150,000 aircraft a year.

The whole complex is true to the Italian flair for architecture and design. The terminal buildings have long, uncluttered lines outside and are tastefully appointed within. As Alitalia, Italy's national airline, was involved in the initial planning of the airport, many of the facilities are designed with the airline and its passengers in mind. There is an impressive feeling of space at Leonardo da Vinci but every bit of it will be needed if the passenger flow continues to increase at the rate it has done since the airport opened in 1961. From 2,000,000 then the figure has now leapt to over 10,000,000, which has necessitated the planning and building of new facilities.

Not every city in need of an international airport has the facilities actually to accommodate one. However superb the designs may be in theory and however much money can be raised to build it, there is always the problem of where actually to put it. An international airport requires a minimum of 40 km² (15½ square miles) of land but 80 km² is a more realistic figure. Some can manage with less, some like London Gatwick and Toronto cover as much as 57 km² (22 square miles). Absurd situations arise where an airport has the space to expand, as Gatwick does, but cannot obtain the planning permission to build. A city can no longer function and expand commercially today if it is cut off from the outside world. This is particularly true of places like Hong Kong and Singapore.

Since the last war Hong Kong and Singapore have become the commercial and financial centres of the East and an airport for each is an absolute necessity. But where does one build an airport with a runway capable of handling the big jets in a tiny colony like Hong Kong, packed with people and buildings and ringed by mountains and sea? The answer, quite simply, is if it cannot be built on land, then it has to be built on water. The Kai Tak project was undertaken in the mid-1950s. It required nearly $130,000,000 and millions of tons of rubble, concrete and other materials to build a foundation out into Kowloon Bay that could tolerate aircraft weights of up to 200,000 kg (450,000 lb). The runway has since been extended to accommodate all the current jet aircraft, including the Boeing 747.

Kai Tak is one of the busiest cargo ports in the East and plans are already going ahead to relieve the ever increasing pressure of traffic by building a replacement. The airport buildings are conventional in design and would look out of place against the surrounding mountains if it were not for the tower blocks, hotels and offices of Hong Kong itself. Kai Tak is home base for Cathay Pacific Airlines and a destination point for many of the world's largest airlines.

# Airport of the future

Another location with very similar problems to Hong Kong is Singapore. It is a very small island with a huge business turnover in exported goods, banking, finance, insurance and oil. Singapore is one of the busiest seaports in the world and during the past 12 years its role as a commercial centre has become recognised throughout the world. Currently there is one airport functioning to capacity at Paya Lebar, but a new one is about to be opened which should relieve the ever-increasing burden of air traffic on the island.

An estimated S$1,723,000,000 is being spent to make Changi one of the finest airports in the world. It will be fully operational by 1983 and has been designed to cope with traffic well into the 21st century. It is just 20 minutes by highway from the city and will be four times the size of the existing airport at Paya Lebar. Of the 16 km² (6 square mile) site, 9 km² (3½ square miles) is reclaimed land. Much of the work has already been completed, including a 4,000 m (4,374 yd) runway, one of two massive runways planned for the airport. The second one will be 3,355 m (3,669 yd) and 60 m (65 yd) wide on reclaimed land. Take-off and approach will be mainly over the sea. There are 45 parking bays with facilities for ten more, to accommodate every type of aircraft including the wide-bodied jets and Concorde. Singapore Airways will fly the British Airways Concorde in from Bahrain on the regular scheduled flights already in operation to Singapore.

Passenger facilities have been given equal priority with aircraft and the terminal area will be vast. Five storeys covering 220,000 m² (263,000 sq yd) will cope with 10,000,000 passengers a year. Baggage handling, security and passenger services are of the most modern design and computerized information display systems have been installed. Cargo is also becoming very big business for Singapore and 925 vehicle parking lots with separate access

roads are being included in the plan. Forecasts estimate 500,000 tons of cargo will be handled by 1986.

In-flight catering is being accommodated on the same scale and a new centre will produce up to 30,000 meals a day, rising to 50,000 by 1986. Singapore Airlines, who have a reputation for outstanding service and first-class catering aboard their aircraft, are deeply involved with these facilities. They are also constructing a vast aircraft maintenance facility, which, when completed, will be the world's largest pillar-free hangar, with a ground area equivalent to seven football pitches. Singapore Airlines have spent S$178,000,000 on the new hangar, which includes extensive parts and spares storage, excellent fire-fighting equipment and first-class staff facilities. Emergency services at Changi include the latest in super foam tenders, command and rapid intervention vehicles. There are sophisticated radar and navigational installations and a fully automated traffic control centre costing S$32,000,000. All these things taken together will make Changi one of the world's most advanced airports.

Another airport-by-the-sea in the shadow of a mountain is Rio de Janeiro. Brazil, however, is more fortunate than Hong Kong or Singapore, in that space does not cause too much of a problem. The newer Galeao international airport is built on the site of a much older one, using many of the original features to good advantage. The passenger terminals are semi-circular in shape, similar to those at Dallas-Fort Worth, with the aircraft parking bays ranged along the outside edge of the circle. There is one runway currently in use, with a second under construction and a third one on the design sheet for when it is required. One notable feature of the Galeao design is built-in room for expansion within the airport itself. The terminals and car-parking area have been laid out in such a way as to allow areas to be filled in with terminal extensions or extra storeys of car park as required. The landing system comprises the most modern equipment available and the facilities are suitable for all aircraft including Concorde, which flies in on a sheduled Air France service from Paris.

A new airport can be a controversial subject – in fact, any airport can arouse controversy. But the prospect of building one within the vicinity of human habitation seems to rouse the man in the street to excesses of passion and rebellion. Of the new generation of modern airports built during the past few years none has aroused so much feeling as Tokyo's Narita. Although it was begun nearly ten years ago, the actual opening of the airport was held up for several years while airport authorities did battle with some of the fiercest protests ever encountered. The building of Narita excited more opposition and violent anti-airport demonstrations than any other airport, before or since. Political and public opinion was inflamed by the media until there were serious doubts as to whether the airport could be operated at all. Stories of the traditionally calm and progressive-minded Japanese hurling petrol bombs in protest were reported in the Western press, while passengers reported being searched as many as five times during their passage through the airport.

When the airport finally opened in 1978, it gave invaluable relief to Haneda, the original airport, which had reached saturation point. Passenger flow and facilities have been carefully designed at Narita to avoid the chaos at Haneda. At present there are two satellite terminals and one runway, with provision for two more. The architecture of the airport buildings is 'office block' in style and not particularly attractive but it does have a look of functional importance. Japanese Air Lines (JAL) have extensive facilities at Narita and have taken advantage of the opportunity of establishing a new base as Singapore Airlines have done at Changi. Narita lies about 65 km (40 miles) east of Tokyo. Because of the distance, a high-speed monorail train has been considered although this is still in the prototype stage.

Some of the major international airports, for all their sophisticated traffic control equipment, passenger flow systems and mobile lounges, are singularly unspectacular to look at. In fact, in some cases the arriving business executive probably feels he is walking into a replica of his own office block. There are, naturally, the space-age exceptions

to this rule, some of which have been mentioned. There are also a handful of superb airport buildings which have been designed from a completely different approach. These have incorporated the true flavour of the countries they serve and have developed the traditional style of the native architecture.

# Jewel of the desert

One of the finest examples is the Arab Emirate airport of Sharjah. The terminal is a complex of circular, domed, mosque-like buildings in brilliant white, connected by covered access ways. The control tower, at one end, is a smooth and elegant bulb on a tall white stem. The whole impression in the dazzling sunshine is more of a millionaire's desert retreat in the guise of a religious shrine, with palm trees scattered about the garden areas around the terminals. Aircraft look singularly out of place against this timeless feat of architecture which is far more suited to Lawrence and his camel.

Sharjah has three terminals in one connected complex and one runway in operation at present. Although the obvious role of a new airport is a centre for business travellers, there are great hopes that Sharjah will be equally successful as a port for the growing tourist trade. It is conveniently situated very near the city of Sharjah and is capable of handling all current narrow and wide-bodied jets.

The Middle East is justly proud of its airports. They are without doubt amongst the finest-looking anywhere in

the world. The United Arab Emirates can boast more than one outstanding example of airport architecture. As well as Sharjah there is also Dubai and Abu Dhabi, totally different in layout and design, but still echoing the flavour of the East. The terminal at Dubai International is oblong in shape, with a flat roof supported by slender white pillars which fan out into inverted umbrella-shaped capitals. Like Sharjah, the building is white with four piers of matching design to blend in with the overall effect. The terminal has been extended and a second one is to be built, as well as a second runway, to relieve the one currently in operation. Dubai International is only a short distance from the city of Dubai and 20 km (12 miles) from Sharjah.

Sharjah embodies the traditional, Dubai gives a modern interpretation to the ancient theme, but Abu Dhabi is unashamedly modern. However, despite this it still retains an intangible distinctiveness which typifies the airports of the Gulf and makes them unique. The single terminal is a white, three-storey building built by a British construction company. The airport itself is managed by another British company, International Aeradio Limited, who give similar services, to various authorities around the world including the supply of air traffic control equipment. There is one runway currently in use at Abu Dhabi handling about 50,000 aircraft movements a year. A new airport is soon to open which will eventually share the load of traffic currently handled by Abu Dhabi International.

*Efficient and very busy – Schiphol, one of the gateways to Europe.*

# The Airport Terminal

Airport terminals range from the most primitive to the most exotic. Much depends on when the terminal was built and the purpose it was intended to serve. Some airport authorities prefer the cold, functional and efficient look of Schiphol, Frankfurt and Heathrow. Others use considerable imagination and employ creative architects to welcome the passenger, either with futuristic structures like the Saarinen terminal at Dulles or with superbly tasteful and attractive buildings such as those at Dubai, Abu Dhabi and Sharjah International in the United Arab Emirates.

Whatever the look of the place it still has a very important role to fulfil, and experienced passengers will know to their cost that the best-looking terminal is not necessarily the most efficient. With 20–30,000,000 passengers passing through every year the airport terminal must be designed to cope not only with current traffic, but with however much there may be in 10 or even 20 years' time. There is no future in building an extra runway if there is nowhere to park the extra aircraft, and there is no point in building additional parking facilities if there is no terminal to handle the additional number of passengers. The daily arrivals need only be increased by five 747 flights to boost the passenger load by 2,000 a day.

Different airport authorities have their own ideas but generally the same principles apply to every international airport. In fact, one of the biggest complaints about airports is their lack of identity. Some airlines have tried to combat this image by introducing special features such as sari-clad stewardesses on Air-India or Elizabethan menus on British Airways flights across the Atlantic. It is more difficult to introduce any local colour to a building which must by definition be 'international'. Perhaps the most successful attempts have been those of the United Arab Emirate airports discussed earlier.

Passengers will generally arrive at the airport by road, rail or helicopter. If arriving by road, the traveller will want somewhere to park his car. Most airports have short-term car parks close to the terminal with baggage trolleys available for suitcases. London Gatwick is well designed from this point of view. Passengers have only a short walk under cover to reach the terminal without having to brave the English weather. The long-term parks are more distant and passengers and their baggage are ferried to the terminal in mini-buses. Because space is almost invariably at a premium, multi-storey car parks are usually favoured although, for some reason, very few airports go for underground facilities.

The passenger enters the terminal through automatic doors. These are almost always used since the majority of people passing through them will be loaded down with bags and cases. Once inside, the first item on the agenda is to check in. In a large airport there may be dozens of airlines running regular scheduled services and all represented with their own check-in desks. These will be identified by signs and by the airline's insignia prominently displayed for the passenger to locate. Some airports in the United States now have curbside baggage check-in desks where the motorist can pull up at the counter with his luggage.

## Checking in

When checking in, the ticket is processed by the airline representative, the passenger is given a boarding card for the aircraft and his baggage is either weighed or counted depending on the airline. There is a maximum weight on some flights over which an excess charge must be paid – usually per kilo. This weight limit does not include hand luggage, which is restricted by the number of items rather than by their weight. This is the last the passenger will see of his baggage until he arrives at his destination where, hopefully, it will reappear for collection.

The designer of an airport terminal has to consider many needs over and above the most obvious ones. Not all the passengers waiting to take off will have arrived fresh from home. Many will have already flown a considerable distance and be waiting to make a connection for another destination. Others may have had a long train journey to reach the airport from the far end of the country. Worst of all, there may be delays caused by bad weather or industrial action, creating queues of waiting passengers that can stretch the airport facilities to the extreme.

*Below International language barriers have been overcome by using symbols indicating the whereabouts of the various facilities and services.*
*Far right Passengers checking in at a typical international terminal.*

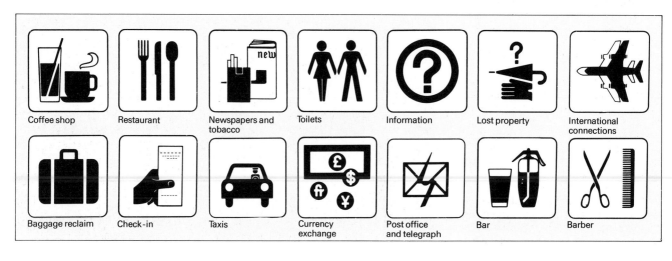

| | | | | | | |
|---|---|---|---|---|---|---|
| Coffee shop | Restaurant | Newspapers and tobacco | Toilets | Information | Lost property | International connections |
| Baggage reclaim | Check-in | Taxis | Currency exchange | Post office and telegraph | Bar | Barber |

As soon as people find themselves in a strange place with time on their hands they invariably want feeding. Restaurant and snack bar facilities are important features of any terminal. Some airports make a focal point of them, none more impressive than the 'space-station' restaurant at Los Angeles which is the airport's main centre of attraction. In addition to several restaurants, there will probably be one or two self-service snack bars and perhaps a Scandinavian cold table or a health food bar to cater for different tastes. At some airports special dietary requirements are also catered for and diabetics, for example, can obtain suitable food.

Most large airports also have several bars and, again, special themes are devised to capture the imagination of the unsuspecting passenger. He may find himself with Hawaiian leis around his neck drinking out of a coconut shell or surrounded by early aircraft memorabilia – if some reports are to be believed. Either way, the bars are fully stocked with every national taste in drink from tequila to ouzo, and the local licensing laws do not always affect the sale of alcohol. Airports are open round the clock and therefore, ideally, the bars and restaurants should stay open too.

As well as food, the passenger may require something to read while he is waiting for his flight. Bookshops and newspaper sales booths hold a wide range of reading matter, including magazines, books and papers in various languages. Besides reading matter there will probably be a selection of items including stationery, small gifts and children's games and toys. Chemists sell toiletries, perfume, sunglasses, make-up and pharmaceutical goods including air sickness tablets. They provide baby food and utensils for nursing mothers and some will also make up prescriptions.

Having made one long journey and with the prospect of another in a few hours time, the passenger may welcome the opportunity to bath or shower. Some airports provide bath or shower facilities where passengers can clean up. Some airports have sauna and massage parlours as well as beauty salons and hairdresssers. There may be rest rooms where passengers can relax and sleep for a few hours before departure. Special facilities are usually provided for nursing mothers where they can wash and change their babies and feed them in privacy. In some cases there is a nurse on duty to assist should any problems arise. Toilets are provided on every floor with facilities for the disabled.

All the services one would expect to find in a big city are concentrated into the airport terminal. There will be a post office where letters can be dispatched, telephone calls made and cables or telexes sent. Some airports provide a poste restante service for passengers expecting messages. There are cloakrooms and sometimes lockers for depositing cumbersome baggage that will not be needed for a few hours. There are usually banks with foreign exchange desks and these are sometimes open 24 hours a day. In fact, there is very little that cannot be bought or acquired within the airport.

## Duty-free

For many passengers, particularly the holidaymakers, the most important place is undoubtedly the duty-free shop. Schiphol, Amsterdam's busy international airport, is reputed to have one of the best duty-free shops of any airport in the world. Some, like the one at Beauvais near Paris, appear to be permanently locked with only a few aging bottles of French perfume in the window covered by a layer of dust. For some people the idea of getting something a little cheaper than usual seems to outweigh the fact that they probably would never have bought it in the first place. Passengers spend millions every year on duty-free goods, making them big businsss for every airport. They also make big business for the customs officers who are kept busy relieving passengers of quantities of items which have tempted them over the limit.

If the passenger is at all nervous or in any doubt as to whether he will ever reach his destination in one piece, he too may be catered for. Some airports sell life insurance – 'good for one flight', to quote a famous American comedian. Some companies have tried slot machines which dispense the policies when the applicant drops in the appropriate number of coins. All this may seem amusing to the hardened traveller but it is a little ominous to the apprehensive flier.

Another facility offered by most airports is a chapel. This is usually inter-denominational, although there may be a separate one for the native religion of the country. In case of an accident or illness there is a medical unit and first aid centre at every airport where passengers can go for treatment. These units have been known to cope with everything from heart attacks to premature births. Some provide vaccinations for passengers who have turned up without the required certificates of inoculation. Passengers arriving from abroad will find general information desks and tourist offices where they can obtain maps and guide books, hotel reservation desks and a selection of car hire companies offering self-drive and chauffeur-driven car services.

If the passenger is still at a loss for something to do he can always go up to the observation deck. Some airports have one for the public as well as the passengers since they provide quite a useful source of additional income. However, security problems have encouraged designers of newer airports to provide large picture windows on the main concourses instead. Some airports charge exorbitant fees to stand and watch the aircraft and it is not always advisable for the passenger about to depart. He is quite likely to see his new Gucci suitcase hurtling across the tarmac on a transporter, buried under about fifty or sixty other cases en route for the aircraft. One passenger at London Heathrow became very alarmed at seeing what she was convinced was her case being loaded on to a British Airways TriStar while waiting to fly to Toronto aboard an Air Canada 747. Not being inclined to make a fuss she crossed her fingers and put her trust in the airline – justifiably as it turned out – thus proving that even the most distinctive suitcase is not unique.

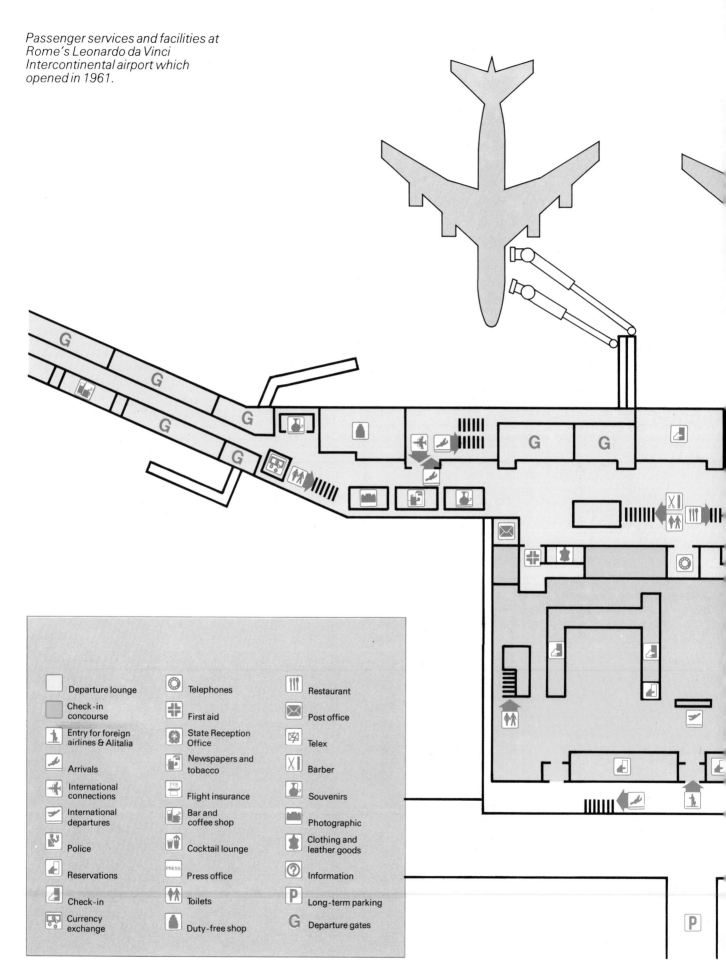

*Passenger services and facilities at Rome's Leonardo da Vinci Intercontinental airport which opened in 1961.*

Departure lounge

Check-in concourse

Entry for foreign airlines & Alitalia

Arrivals

International connections

International departures

Police

Reservations

Check-in

Currency exchange

Telephones

First aid

State Reception Office

Newspapers and tobacco

Flight insurance

Bar and coffee shop

Cocktail lounge

Press office

Toilets

Duty-free shop

Restaurant

Post office

Telex

Barber

Souvenirs

Photographic

Clothing and leather goods

Information

Long-term parking

Departure gates

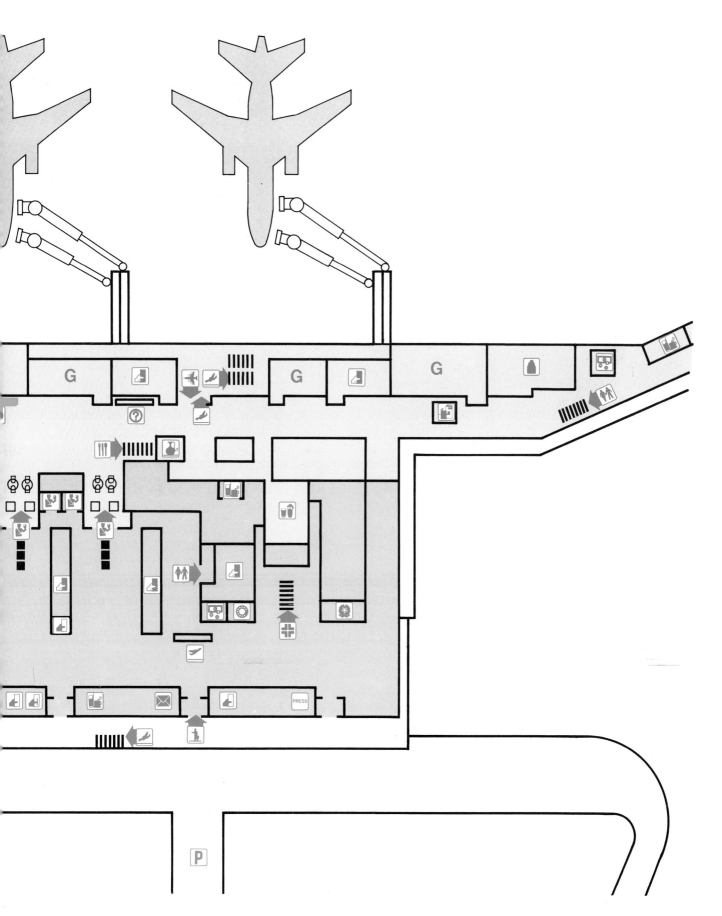

# Passenger Flow

All movement and activity within the confines of the terminal building are watched over from an operations centre. Closed-circuit television helps to monitor the passenger flow and to oversee the various centres of activity. If the layout of the building has been well thought out there should be an uninterrupted flow route for passengers to follow on or off an aircraft without treading on each other's toes.

In an ideal world the passengers would arrive in a constant, even stream with half-hourly breaks for staff to have coffee or tea. In the hard reality of a typical airport, passengers swarm off three 747s at once and flood into the arrivals' area. After this onslaught the officials detect a lull in the arrivals and the human stampede recedes while the staff draw breath for the next peak period. National holidays and summer vacation periods are the nightmare of some of the older, more crowded airports. Bad weather also bodes ill at certain airports, particularly those prone to fog, a climatic condition which has little regard for package holiday charters and holidaymakers.

Ideas on 'passenger flow' have changed over the years, or rather, evolved. In the early days it was not so necessary to herd people on to moving walkways, because the numbers were that much smaller. Today modern terminals are designed not only with current needs in mind but with built-in 'growth potential' to cater for the future. By separating arrival and departure areas the circuitous route from aircraft to taxi, bus or private car is made as simple and as uninterrupted as possible.

## Duty to pay

Passengers leave the aircraft through an airbridge or via a mobile staircase, possibly with a bus to transport them to the arrivals' area. From there, they pass either through a transit lounge for a connecting flight or to passport control. Passports are inspected and health and immigration officers examine vaccination certificates and entry permits. Passengers arriving from countries where serious endemic diseases are prevalent or where an outbreak of serious infection has been reported are examined.

Security and immigration officials keep a constant look-out for undesirable aliens, wanted offenders and blacklisted persons generally.

While this scrutiny is taking place the baggage will have been off-loaded and dispatched by moving ramps to the collection point. The passengers seek, and hopefully find, their baggage before passing through customs. The old maxim of 'breakfast in London, lunch in New York, baggage in Tehran' still holds true for many unfortunate passengers, some airports being more notorious than others for losing luggage. Blame for the loss is usually passed backward and forward between airport baggage-handlers and the airlines. The only advice to be given to the passenger is to be sure that everything is insured. When one considers how many millions of suitcases pour through airports around the world every day it is amazing that more do not go astray.

## 'Deplaning'

Having retrieved their cases, the passengers move on to the customs desks – probably the least popular stop on the journey. Some airports still handle passengers individually but the majority of large airports now use the faster green/red channel system. Customs officers watch from a distance as the passengers filter through the channel of their choice. In theory anyone with goods to declare should choose the red channel and those with nothing to pay duty on should go through the green channel.

Customs officers are probably best described as amateur psychologists. They have years of experience in the study of human behaviour and have become experts in facial expressions and signs of nerves or guilt. Customs officers have some very amusing tales to tell about the public and how they distinguish the amateur 'smuggler'. He falls into two basic categories. There is the unobtrusive, rather nervous type who creeps through the green channel with his eyes fixed firmly on the ground and a half-bottle too much of Scotch in his pocket. A more rewarding catch is the bluff type who barges through, confidently cracking jokes with fellow travellers and officials alike, with a shining new Pentax slung nonchalantly over his shoulder.

In reality the camera or half-bottle of Scotch is small fry for the customs men. Far more interesting is the consignment of heroin, cannabis or cocaine lurking in the most innocent-looking piece of luggage. Drug smugglers are amazingly imaginative when it comes to concealing their merchandise. Hoards have been found welded into the chassis of cars, linings of handbags or suitcases and, on extreme occasions, even packed into a condom and swallowed by the smuggler at the last minute. Certain flights are more suspect than others for drug smuggling. Passengers arriving from the Far East and North Africa are carefully screened, while departures for South America and the Middle East are favourites for gun-runners.

In this automatic age passengers get very little exercise at an airport. Leg work is reduced to a minimum with moving pavements, escalators, lifts, mobile lounges and buses to ferry people and baggage in and out of the terminal. For departing passengers the flow works in the same way but in reverse. Although most countries are more concerned about what comes in than what goes out, there is a constant watch kept for wanted individuals, trying to beat a hasty retreat from the law. All departing passengers are screened by X-ray equipment and metal detectors that are used for picking up firearms. A well-known American personality had his 'gorillas' stopped at one European airport for displaying suspiciously large bulges under their left armpits.

Passengers check in at the appropriate airline desk and have their baggage checked. This is the last they will see of it until they and the baggage, hopefully, reach the same destination. If by chance a baggage trolley is spotted on its way out to the aircraft, the experienced passenger will quickly avert his gaze. It is bad enough to see your best suitcase crushed under a dozen others, but it is even worse when you can't see it at all!

Once the tickets have been checked and the baggage taken care of, passengers can sit in the departure lounge and amuse themselves for as many minutes, hours or days as they will have to wait. Flights from most airports are fairly punctual within a margin of about half an hour. During the holiday season it is harder to keep to schedule to the minute, and airports with restricted runway and terminal facilities such as London Gatwick do suffer from delays during peak periods. The two perils which beset the majority of airports at some time or another are fog and industrial disputes. Air traffic controllers have been particularly militant during the late 1970s and have wreaked havoc with holiday flights in Europe. Within hours the spacious concourse of a large terminal can become like a refugee centre.

## Departures

A large number of passengers arrive convinced that their flight will be delayed anyway. Seasoned travellers will know that congestion has probably held up an incoming aircraft – nervous fliers will be convinced that engineers are busy trying to stick a wing back on. First-class passengers have a much easier time all round. They merit special check-in facilities and do not usually have to appear until the flight is near departure. Concorde passengers get their own VIP treatment, with a separate lounge and check-in area. Concorde departure from London Heathrow is even signposted on the approach roads.

## 'Flight number…'

If the airport is true to the great tradition, a bleep over the public address system will introduce an unintelligible announcement in several different languages. Usually the only words easily defined are 'flight number . . .'. It may be unfair to accuse every airport of this, but it is still the case with far too many. The real problems seem to arise when a flight leaving London for Tokyo has to be announced by someone whose Japanese is poor. The English-speaking world probably does not fully appreciate this because their language is virtually international, certainly in the airline business.

The most comprehensible way of conveying information is by closed-circuit television linked to a computer or by the use of a large Solari sign board similar to those used in railway terminals. This can be updated as flights arrive and depart, and passengers can see their particular flight at a glance. As it moves up the list towards the top they can see how near it is to departure. Alongside the flight number there is a word of instruction such as 'boarding' or 'last call'. This system has been adopted by nearly every international airport and screens are positioned all over the terminal building.

Once called, the passengers pass through the security checks and metal detectors. An airline employee checks the boarding cards while passengers assemble ready to be taken out to the aircraft. Some airports still make their passengers walk, if only up a mobile staircase. Others have introduced the mobile lounge, which must be the ultimate in luxury or laziness – depending on how one sees it. Passengers arrive at the boarding gate and sit down in comfortable chairs in the 'lounge'. When the moment for departure arrives a door is closed and the whole lounge area drives off, passengers and all. When it reaches the aircraft a door at the other end is opened and the cargo of people step straight into the aircraft and sit down again.

The cabin crew welcome each passenger aboard with that flashing airline smile unique to members of their profession and conduct anything up to 400 people plus hand luggage to their seats. Everyone is strapped in and the doors are secured ready for take off. The seasoned traveller can now relax. The nervous one can start worrying.

*Passengers check in at London Heathrow for Singapore Airlines flights from Terminal 3 which handles all international traffic.*

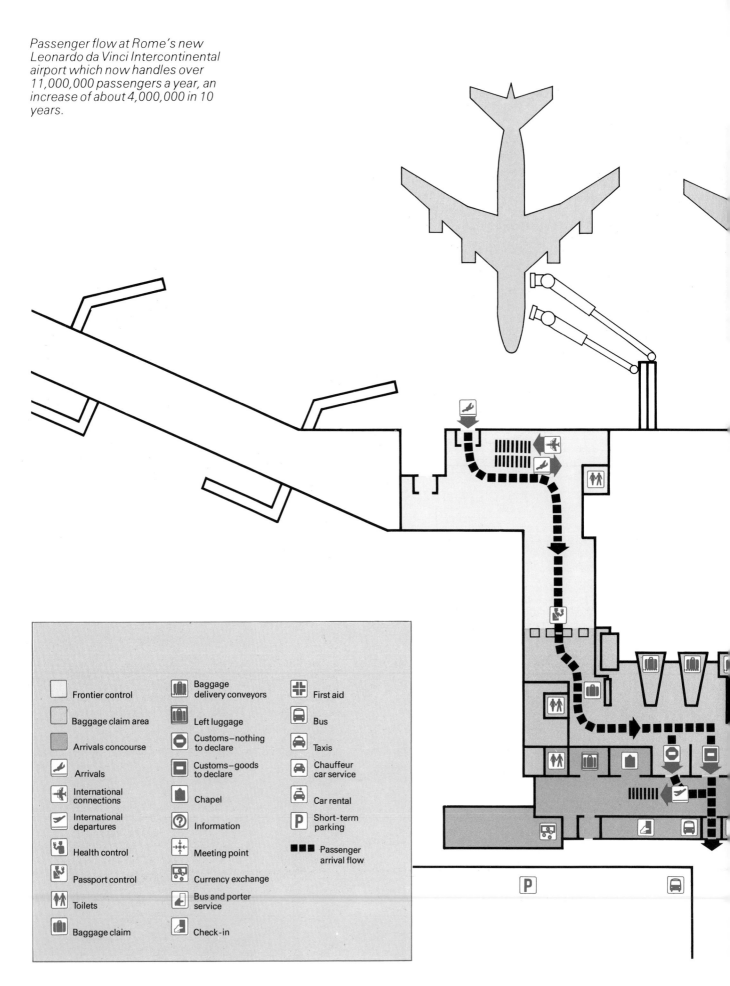

Passenger flow at Rome's new
Leonardo da Vinci Intercontinental
airport which now handles over
11,000,000 passengers a year, an
increase of about 4,000,000 in 10
years.

| | | |
|---|---|---|
| Frontier control | Baggage delivery conveyors | First aid |
| Baggage claim area | Left luggage | Bus |
| Arrivals concourse | Customs—nothing to declare | Taxis |
| Arrivals | Customs—goods to declare | Chauffeur car service |
| International connections | Chapel | Car rental |
| International departures | Information | Short-term parking |
| Health control | Meeting point | Passenger arrival flow |
| Passport control | Currency exchange | |
| Toilets | Bus and porter service | |
| Baggage claim | Check-in | |

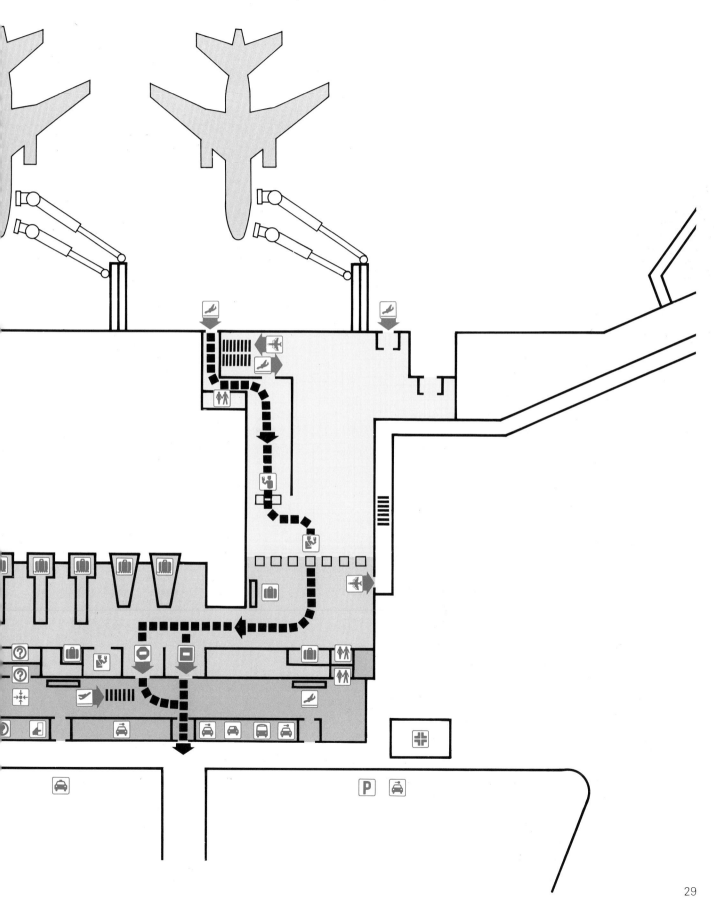

*The Big Orange, Braniff's now-famous 747 which flies the Atlantic regularly to London Gatwick.*

# Ground Services

# Ground Vehicles

For every aircraft passing through an international airport there are twice as many ground vehicles giving vital back-up support. Many of them are specially designed and built for specific purposes relating to the aircraft, the passengers, baggage, catering, runway maintenance, fire and security. In addition to these specialized vehicles there are conventional cars, jeeps and trucks painted in a bright colour. They are usually yellow and are clearly marked for identification.

The easiest to spot are the 'follow me's'. These are usually small trucks or jeeps with a large sign on the back quite simply telling the aircraft to 'follow me'. Their job is to guide a taxiing aircraft into the appropriate parking bay. Jeeps are also used for checking the runways for debris and patches of rubber. They cruise the length of each runway at regular intervals or are used to make an inspection if a pilot reports some obstruction on landing or take-off. A bumpy landing or a slight skid can leave patches of rubber from the aircraft's tyres on the surface of the runway. If left to accumulate too long this deposited rubber makes a very slippery surface on a wet day, so an inspection team is sent out to view it at regular intervals.

For the more specialized jobs around the airport there are fleets of vehicles with every combination of ramps, lifting devices and telescopic arms and legs. When an aircraft is required and it is not already in the parking bay, it will need to be towed from the maintenance hangar. For this purpose there are heavy four-wheel-drive 'tugs'. The largest and most powerful of these looks exactly like a big, flat box on wheels. These tugs are capable of towing a 747 weighing more than 360,000 kg (800,000 lb). There are also smaller, lighter versions which can tow weights of up to 45,000 kg (100,000 lb) at a speed of around 10 km/h (6 mph) in bottom gear. This is the equivalent in weight of a DC-9 or a BAC One-Eleven. The speed at which a tug can pull an aircraft depends on the weight it is towing, but the maximum is around 30 km/h (20 mph) in top gear. Conventional tugs have a vertical tow-

Above *A Houchin Model 604 ground power unit stands beside a Dan-Air 727.*
Right *A scissor-lift catering hoist loading a Chinese Airlines 707.*

bar which is connected by a towing arm to the nosewheel of the aircraft, but there are now fast-moving tugs at certain airports which can actually carry the nosewheel, mounted on a special platform. One over-enthusiastic tug driver attempted to make off with an HS748 at Charles de Gaulle airport in Paris, before the pilot had released the brakes. The nose gear collapsed and the tug became embedded in the fuselage of the aircraft, causing substantial damage to both.

## Turn-around

Once the aircraft has been towed into the parking bay a swarm of other vehicles descend on various missions. The aircraft must be refuelled before take-off, either from a tanker fitted with a special boom to reach the fuel inlet or from a hydrant on the parking apron. Where an airport has a 'fuel farm' nearby, hydrants can be located at convenient intervals in the parking area. A dispenser vehicle, which is simply a

Right *Cargo being loaded on to an Alitalia DC-10 at Leonardo da Vinci Intercontinental airport.*
Below *Houchin pneumatic starter unit supplies 55 kg (120 lb) of low pressure air per minute.*

pump on wheels, is connected to the hydrant and pumps fuel directly into the aircraft, avoiding the hazards of ferrying thousands of gallons of highly volatile fuel around in tankers. John F. Kennedy has the largest fuel farm in the world, holding 114,000,000 litres (25,000,000 gal) at any one time.

While the re-fuelling is going on, catering and supply vehicles will be busy restocking the galleys, cabins and toilets, ready for the next load of passengers. The cleaners and catering staff are ferried out to the aircraft in special transporters. The body of the transporter is on hydraulic legs which can be raised to the level of the door in the side of the aircraft. The food, drink, tableware, linen and other necessities are packed into containers and the whole package delivered to the aircraft on a six-wheeled 'catering hoist'. The hoist can raise its load 5 m (18 ft) into the air, level with the door of a 747. British Airways alone have 36 of these vehicles to ensure fast turn-around for the busy domestic and transatlantic fleet.

Food is not the only essential to be loaded each time a flight is prepared for. There must be water, both for drinking and for toilet purposes. Water is delivered in supply trucks which can carry over 2,700 litres (600 gal). These trucks can refill an aircraft at a rate of 45 litres (10 gal) a minute. The self-propelled toilet servicing units also have a capacity

*A heavy-duty tug prepares to tow a very much larger British Airways 747 by its nose gear.*

of up to 2,700 litres (600 gal) and the toilet water units hold up to 4,100 litres (900 gal) at one time.

For carrying out routine checks and maintenance there are special platforms on wheels, with a telescopic gantry which can be raised to the required height. These are used for inspecting the engines and flying controls of an aircraft on the ground. For reaching the less accessible parts of the fuselage for cleaning and maintenance there are long extendable platforms similar to those used for repairing street lights.

To pay their way, aircraft must fly as often as possible and as full as possible. They must not only be full of passengers but full of cargo as well. Before the passengers board, any air cargo must be loaded on double-decker loading platforms. These are particularly efficient for loading large-capacity aircraft such as the 747. The twin platforms are used alternately. One is raised to carry cargo to the door of the aircraft while the other is being loaded with the next pallets or containers. The loaded platform is then hoisted up to be unloaded while the empty one is lowered back to the ground for yet another load. For lighter or less bulky items there are fork-lift trucks which can be manoeuvred quickly around the aircraft.

## Loading up

All is now ready for the passengers. The aircraft has been cleaned, new supplies of food, drink, crockery, linen and toiletries are aboard, the tanks are full of fuel and the cargo hold is being loaded with the passengers' baggage. Few passengers seem to appreciate what a rough time a fragile or badly-made suitcase can have at the hands of the baggage loaders — both human and mechanical. There is no time carefully to lift each individual case and deposit it gently in the aircraft. All too often a handsome-looking executive suitcase will end up in two halves on the tarmac, leaving a trail of underwear and personal belongings behind it. A good, sturdy case, preferably with straps round it, is far more likely to make it along the baggage conveyor and up into the aircraft. The conveyor itself is a continuous belt of rubber on a metal frame which can be raised to the height of the cargo door.

*Left An El Al 707 sits on the tarmac surrounded by activity as passengers begin boarding. Many airports now have covered airbridges.*

The passengers are the last to arrive and whether they arrive seated or on foot depends on the airport facilities. At the more modern airport terminals expandable concertina-like tubes fit against the side of the aircraft. Passengers can walk through these and board without having to step outside. This system is particularly useful in countries where the climate produces unfavourable weather conditions. Airports in the United States have pioneered the 'mobile lounge' described earlier.

For those passengers who still have to walk there are self-propelled staircases which can be adjusted according to the height of the aircraft. These come in various designs, some with canopies, some without. Self-propelled types are mounted on to the rear of a small truck, while others are towed. The insignia of the airline that uses them is usually displayed on the side.

With everything loaded, the passengers in their seats and the flight crew aboard at the controls, it only remains for the engines to be started and for the aircraft to taxi on to the runway. Aircraft do not have built-in starter motors in quite the same way motor cars do. The engines need to be 'cranked' by an independent ground starter unit. A controlled flow of low pressure air is supplied to the engine, powered by a diesel engine coupled to a compressor. The units are mounted on a chassis for towing with a built-in fuel tank which carries 200 litres (44 gal).

Finally, the engines are started and all the vehicles retreat to allow the aircraft to taxi out of the parking area. There is no reverse gear on a jet aircraft so a tug must give a 'push back' out of the parking bay. The tug tows the aircraft by the nose gear and positions it on the taxiway. From there the aircraft is on its own, self-sufficient until it lands at its destination.

*Swissair and KLM DC-8s on the tarmac at John F. Kennedy.*

# Fuel

An engine cannot function without fuel and the jet engine is no exception. A fully fuelled 747 can hold 200,000 litres (44,000 gal) of jet fuel weighing around 160,000 kg (157 tons). Jet aircraft use one of two types of oil-derived fuel known as JP1 and JP4. Some engines can run on either with no adjustments; others can be reset for an alternative.

Storing fuel in sufficient quantities to supply the needs of a busy international airport can present a headache for the planners. Where there is a severe lack of space and a close proximity of private homes and offices, finding somewhere to keep the fuel can be quite a problem. At one time tankers could cope quite easily with the job of refuelling aircraft for take off by simply driving up to them and pumping the fuel in. The average tanker used to carry about 2,700 litres (600 gal) which would require 73 of them to refuel a 747. Giant super-tankers do exist but these are not the ideal solution to the problem any more than swarms of smaller ones. It is quite possible to have a dozen 747s parked at any one time and the resulting situation would become chaotic.

The best solution is to have a network of hydrants positioned in each parking bay connected by pipelines to a bulk fuel reserve, usually located away from the aircraft parking areas and known as a 'fuel farm'. The only auxilliary vehicle required is a mobile pump to transfer the fuel into the aircraft's tanks. A wide-bodied jet can be refuelled in half an hour by the hydrant system. The fuel supply is kept replenished at the fuel farm so that there is never any need for tankers to enter the central parking area at all. Apart from the obvious benefits to ground control of having fewer vehicles moving about around the aircraft, it is easier to maintain the correct temperature levels for the fuel. This is particularly important in tropical climates or in very cold conditions. Fuel must never be allowed to boil or freeze. Special insulation lines each tank to maintain a safe temperature.

The fuel farm is obviously a desirable solution to the problems of fuel storage but it requires a great deal of space and can incur the wrath of local residents. A remote, deserted piece of waste land far from human habitation is the ideal location, but few airports are fortunate enough to have such an area on their doorstep. John F. Kennedy airport has the largest fuel farm in the world. It holds 114,000,000 litres (25,000,000 gal) at any one time – enough to refuel about 600 Boeing 747s.

The quantity of fuel an aircraft uses can depend to a certain extent on the pilot. All jets are thirsty – some more so than others – but the biggest are not always the ones to swallow the most fuel. A 747 is relatively economical per passenger km per litre compared with a BAC One-Eleven, which is only two thirds as economical, and Concorde, which is only half as economical. The speed at which fuel is used is referred to as the 'burn rate' and this is quoted in litres per minute. A pilot can make a large dent in his fuel supply simply by 'bad driving'. Flying too fast is inefficient because of the extra drag incurred. Fly-

Right *Refuelling one of the port wing tanks of a Boeing 747.*
Below *Arrangement of fuel tanks on the L-1011 TriStar.*

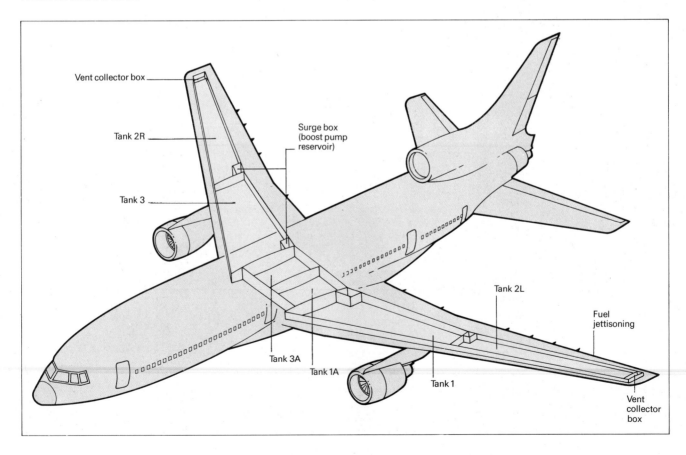

ing too slowly is inefficient and also wastes fuel. In fact, the speed at which the jet engine can propel an aircraft is the only real justification for its using the amount of fuel it does.

## Fuel economy

Not all fuel economies are down to the pilot. A clean aircraft saves fuel. Dirt on the fuselage creates drag which in turn puts a strain on the engines and more fuel is then required to maintain speed. Traffic control may require an aircraft to hold for some time at an uneconomical speed and altitude. A 707 travelling at 18,000 ft on a 1,600 km (1,000 mile) journey will burn up 4,100 litres (900 gal) more fuel than at 35,000 ft over the same distance. The journey will also take three-quarters of an hour longer. Concorde will burn up to 295 litres (65 gal) a minute while it is holding on the stack awaiting permission to land.

Aircraft do not have one fuel tank in the way that a motor car does. Instead, they have several integral tanks which are formed by the wing and fuselage structures. The most common place for fuel storage is in the wing section. The 707 has a series of lined and sealed tanks filling the entire wing section. A central tank is positioned between the wings, with main tanks in the body of each wing and reserve tanks in each wing tip. The main tanks are numbered and the flight engineer can switch from one to another as the supply in each falls. A rare pilot error is to switch to a tank which is already empty, causing the engines to run out of fuel.

## Fuel transfer

As the fuel is burned, so the aircraft becomes lighter and more economical to fly. This can make a weight difference

*Refuelling a Wardair 747 at Gatwick Airport. The refuelling point is located behind one of the four shining General Electric CF6 engines fitted on this particular aircraft.*

of well over 100,000 kg (100 tons) on the 747. However, Concorde puts its fuel load to very good use. Apart from the use of 'elevons' on the wing trailing edges, the trim of the aircraft is maintained by the distribution of the fuel load. The fuel transfer system is an ingenious way of adjusting the centre of gravity of the aircraft by moving fuel from one end of the fuselage to the other. By pumping it backwards and forwards from the central tanks to front and rear trim tanks the weight distribution can be altered in flight.

*The huge 'buckets' of the Olympus engine variable geometry exhaust system are clearly visible in this view of a Concorde taking on a fresh load of fuel.*

The Concorde system differs from the conventional subsonic aircraft system, which uses the fuel in a manner that merely maintains the centre of gravity within acceptable limits. A system of valves and pipes allows the fuel to continue flowing evenly to the engine at whatever angle the aircraft is flying. Civil aircraft do not fly upside down as a rule but military aircraft do and this requires a special system designed to ensure a constant, uninterrupted flow of fuel to the engines. Baffles set inside the tanks prevent the fuel from splashing about. The fuel is pumped from the tanks to the engines by high-pressure pumps. Where there is more than one engine, in some of the later types, the fuel is distributed to each in the correct quantity by a system of proportioners.

Temperature is an important factor in storing fuel aboard an aircraft. If it falls below −40°C (−40°F) or −60°C (−76°F) depending on the types of fuel – there is a danger of lumps forming in the tanks. If water is allowed into the fuel this will freeze at high altitude, causing obstructions in the supply system. Excessively high temperatures are equally undesirable because they cause loss of fuel by evaporation and can also damage valves and seals.

London Heathrow uses more than 10,000,000 litres (2,200,000 gal) of fuel per day, while an airport like Chicago O'Hare uses considerably more. Yet for all the thousands of aircraft moving about daily in and out of hundreds of airports around the world, civil air transport still accounts for less than 5% of the world's entire annual oil-derived fuel consumption.

# Ground Alert

If an accident occurs there is a very good chance that it will happen within sight of the airport. Three out of every four major incidents occur within 800 m (½ mile) of the runway or actually on it. Landing and take-off are the highest risk manoeuvres an aircraft makes and some of the worst accidents have occurred before the aircraft has even left the ground. The current official view is that while approach and landing is still the most hazardous phase of the flight the number of take-off incidents has virtually trebled, indicating an area worthy of much closer scrutiny.

The most horrific fatality involving take-off was the well-reported Tenerife disaster when a KLM 747 collided with a Pan American 747 while taking off for Las Palmas in poor visibility. The Pan Am Aircraft was taxiing across the runway at the time. The KLM hit it and both aircraft caught fire. Two hundred and thirty four passengers and 14 crew died

aboard the Dutch aircraft and 318 plus 9 crew aboard the American one. Both aircraft were completely destroyed.

Thankfully, accidents on this scale are comparatively rare, but they do emphasize the hazards of carrying large numbers of passengers aboard a single aircraft if an accident does occur. The fact that both aircraft at Tenerife caught fire accounted for the high casualty figures. Yet fires are comparatively rare today. Strict international regulations stipulate minimum fire-fighting standards for all airports. Those failing to maintain them would not be permitted to operate.

No emergency is too small to merit turning out the fire services, and the slightest indication of trouble will put the emergency vehicles on stand-by alert. A pilot may detect a minor failure in the hydraulic system, an engine might

lose power or a warning light might come on unexpectedly. Nothing is too small to be ignored when the lives of 400 passengers and millions of dollars worth of aircraft are at stake. Heathrow goes on full emergency alert, on average, once every day of the year. Very few of these alerts turn out to be anything serious and many are false alarms. The most common problems are burst tyres, smoke coming from places it shouldn't and landing gear troubles.

An aircraft carrying 180,000 litres (40,000 gal) of highly volatile jet fuel is a potential bonfire on wheels. The textiles used aboard the aircraft, in the cabin and for upholstery have to be certified as

flame-resistant material, to reduce the risk of fire spreading inside. On the ground a fleet of specially designed fire-fighting vehicles is equipped not only to put out a fire but to prevent it from starting in the first place. Some airports are more adequately equipped than others in this respect and, although they all comply with the regulations in theory, criticism has been levelled at various older airports for not updating their equipment to cater for wide-bodied jets. The new S$1,723,000,000 Changi airport in Singapore is being equipped with an impressive fleet of first-rate vehicles and equipment, including four super foam tenders, rapid intervention vehicles, a fire tender, hydraulic platform and two fire boats.

*Vehicles such as this can expect to be put on alert at least once every day at an international airport.*

# Emergency fleet

A typical emergency fleet is made up of heavy-duty water and foam tenders, medical units and ambulances, lifting and cutting gear for rescue, and lighting for night work. Airports today use rapid intervention vehicles (RIVs). These are capable of arriving on the scene within minutes from stations around the airport. They are fast and manoeuvrable and can race across both grass and concrete. They must be able to cross even the roughest ground to reach the scene of the accident by the most direct route.

The main deterrent for burning fuel is foam, although its usefulness is now subject to debate and some airports tend not to use it any more. Tenders equipped with monitor and hand-held nozzles can deliver more than 5,000 litres (1,100 gal) a minute. The foam itself is mixed with water from a 5,500 litre (1,210 gal) reservoir and is propelled by carbon dioxide from cylinders mounted on the chassis of the vehicle. There are different types of foam but the most stable and efficient for suppressing inflammable liquids is protein-based. Certain types such as Nicerol are specially formulated to avoid corrosion to plastics and metal on the aircraft. The foam subdues the flames and prevents recombustion of the fuel.

Above *The Angus Foam Firestreak rapid intervention vehicle (RIV).*

There is also a powder version of the foam tender which works on the same principles. The powder has the effect of extinguishing volume fires and preventing a rise in temperature within the fuselage of the aircraft. This method, called the Biocarbo B2 system, guarantees a constant pressure flow and maximum range for the projection equipment, using carbon dioxide as the propellant. The vehicles themselves are powered by ten-cylinder engines with nine-speed gearboxes for coping with any terrain.

In addition to the heavy-duty vehicles there are light rescue units which also carry powder or foam. These carry teams of fire-fighters wearing fire-proof clothing made of aluminized material and breathing apparatus to overcome fumes and smoke. Aluminium ladders and cutting equipment can also be carried for rescue work.

The way in which a fire is tackled depends on the nature of the emergency. One fairly common incident is landing gear failure. The pilot reports that his landing gear warning light is signalling a malfunction and will ask permission to circle the tower for a visual inspection. Ground control will confirm whether the gear is down. Meanwhile the emergency crew will be taking up positions along the runway in readiness for the pilot's second approach. A bed of foam is sprayed across the runway to subdue any sparks and flames as the aircraft makes a belly landing. The foam suppresses any sparks which might fly up and ignite fuel leaking from ruptured tanks.

Powder is useful for more localized fires on undercarriages, tyres and electrical equipment. Breathing apparatus may have to be worn when using foam and powder together as they produce noxious fumes on contact with one another. To deal with engine fires there are various types of inert vaporizing gases which are very effective for smothering flames.

Comparing the number of incidents with the number of fatal injuries, very few emergencies cause loss of life. Many of these incidents would be amusing were it not for the cost of repairing the aircraft. An HS748 parked at Jersey airport after landing. The pilot shut down the engines and the aircraft rolled gently backwards. Its elevator came to rest against a steel post, causing substantial damage to the tailplane. The pilot had left the parking brake off.

*The new Gloster Saro Javelin heavy foam crash tender, with automatic transmission, can discharge 4,500 litres (990 gal) per minute from its 10,000 litre (2,200 gal) reservoir.*

# Cargo

Air cargo is big business. Flying an aircraft which is only half full is extremely expensive. For his weight, the average passenger takes up an uneconomical amount of space but cargo can be made to fit every nook and cranny in the aircraft. Some aircraft are specifically built for use as freighters; others are convertible for use as either or both. The 747F has a hinged nose which swings up to allow containers to be loaded from the front. Since its introduction, the 747 has revolutionized the whole idea of air cargo. With its vast capacity and long range it has made air freight a far more viable proposition. It has the great advantage over sea transport of speed and safety. Goods, both perishable and fragile, can be transported quickly by air and arrive fresh at their destination within hours instead of weeks.

Air cargo is loaded on pallets or in specially designed containers. It is not enough to pile loads of differently shaped boxes on the floor and leave them to rattle around. The goods are piled on large flat metal pallets and secured with netting to hold them in place. If the goods are particularly valuable or easily damaged they may be covered by an 'igloo', then secured with netting. Bulky loads are packed into individual containers specifically shaped to fit inside the fuselage of the aircraft. These containers are flat bottomed and slab sided, with rounded tops, and can be used either way up to fit into the upper or lower cargo hold of the aircraft. A half-container is also available for smaller consignments. The containers are known by the designation LD, followed by a number according to the type and size of the container and the purpose for which it is designed.

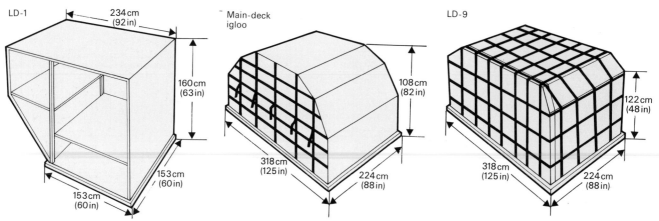

LD-1
234cm (92in)
160cm (63in)
153cm (60in)
153cm (60in)

Main-deck igloo
108cm (82in)
318cm (125in)
224cm (88in)

LD-9
122cm (48in)
318cm (125in)
224cm (88in)

The real economics of air cargo lie in filling up empty space on passenger aircraft that would otherwise be flying half empty, even with a full passenger load. A 747 can still accommodate over 20,000 kg (20 tons) of cargo on the lower deck on pallets or in containers, while carrying its full complement of 400 passengers. The Lockheed L-1011 TriStar will carry over 7,000 kg (7 tons) in addition to its passenger load, and the 707 will carry approximately 6,000 kg (6 tons), although this weight must be loosely packed.

Air cargo has become a fully computerized and highly mechanized business. Airports like Frankfurt, which is the busiest cargo centre in Europe, and John F. Kennedy, which is one of the busiest in the world, are completely automated. There are machines to do every job involved in loading and unloading the aircraft. The cargo is transported to the aircraft or the aircraft goes to the cargo, depending on the facilities at the airport. The big centres have ramps extending from the storage warehouse. These ramps can be loaded at one end with containers, which travel along the ramps straight into the hold of the aircraft parked alongside. Alternatively, there are self-propelled loaders and platforms for moving containers about. The most efficient of these is the scissor-lift type which can be raised to the level of the cargo door. It will remain stable whatever the weight distribution, with no risk of tipping up. Lufthansa uses this type of equipment at the huge Frankfurt cargo terminal at Rhein/Main.

Some airlines have now installed computers which keep track of every consignment passing through. This way advance planning is easier and an uninterrupted flow can be maintained, including regular services such as overseas mail and medical supplies. In addi-

tion to the loading facilities, there must also be substantial warehouse space to store goods awaiting dispatch or collection. Cargo ranges from live animals to radio-active chemicals. Jewels, drink, tobacco, perfume, furs, medical equipment, gold bars and traveller's cheques are all regular customers of the airlines.

With all this valuable cargo awaiting dispatch, security is always a headache for every airline and airport authority. The advent of sealed containers has helped to cut down on pilfering, but the more organized thieves still help themselves to an expensive quantity of goods every year. Some international airports have better reputations than others for security. At some American airports mail is held under guard until it is safely aboard the aircraft and night flights have been abandoned to make the thief's task that much harder. John F. Kennedy is one of the most security-conscious airports and it has shown results, although entire consignments are still known to vanish into 'thin air'.

For cargo the air is a fast and efficient means of transport. Refrigerated containers and special packaging can transport perishables and dangerous chemicals with far less risk than at sea. Urgently needed components and parts can be with a manufacturer within 24 hours, saving weeks. Whole wing sections of aircraft are flown to assembly plants, carefully laid inside an empty 747 or the appropriately-named 'Guppy'. Airbus Industrie uses Super Guppies to fly whole wing and fuselage sections to their plant at Toulouse.

To give some idea of just how big air cargo has become, John F. Kennedy airport handles over 1,200,000 tonnes of cargo a year. Singapore Airlines, who are major cargo carriers in the East, reported that in 1977/78 they reached the 281,000,000 tonne km mark, carrying 52,000 tonnes of cargo. They reckon their cargo capacity has increased by 553% in five years — which is some indication of how rapidly the business of air cargo is growing.

*The ultimate in cargo aircraft — a Super Guppy is loaded with a wing section for an A300 Airbus.*

LD-7

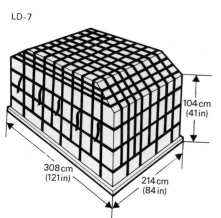

308cm (121in)  214cm (84in)  104cm (41in)

LD-3

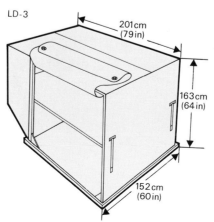

201cm (79in)  163cm (64in)  152cm (60in)

Pallet & net

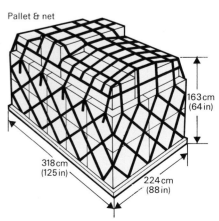

318cm (125in)  224cm (88in)  163cm (64in)

An A300 Airbus makes its final approach, guided in by the landing lights.

# Ground Systems

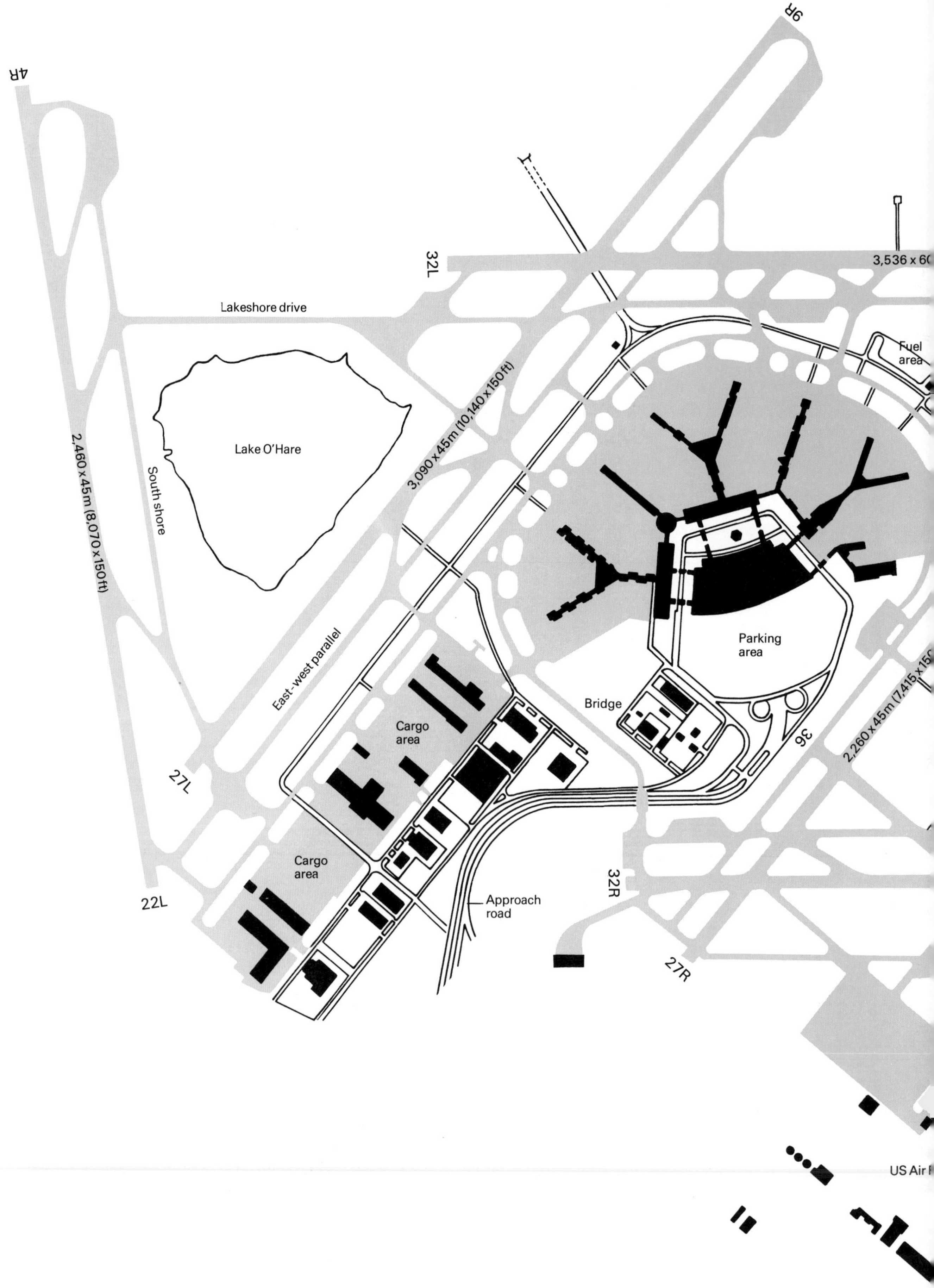

4R

9R

32L

3,536 x 60

Lakeshore drive

Fuel
area

2,460 x 45m (8,070 x 150ft)

South shore

Lake O'Hare

3,090 x 45m (10,140 x 150 ft)

East-west parallel

Parking
area

Bridge

36

2,260 x 45m (7,415 x 150

27L

Cargo
area

Cargo
area

Approach
road

32R

27R

22L

US Air

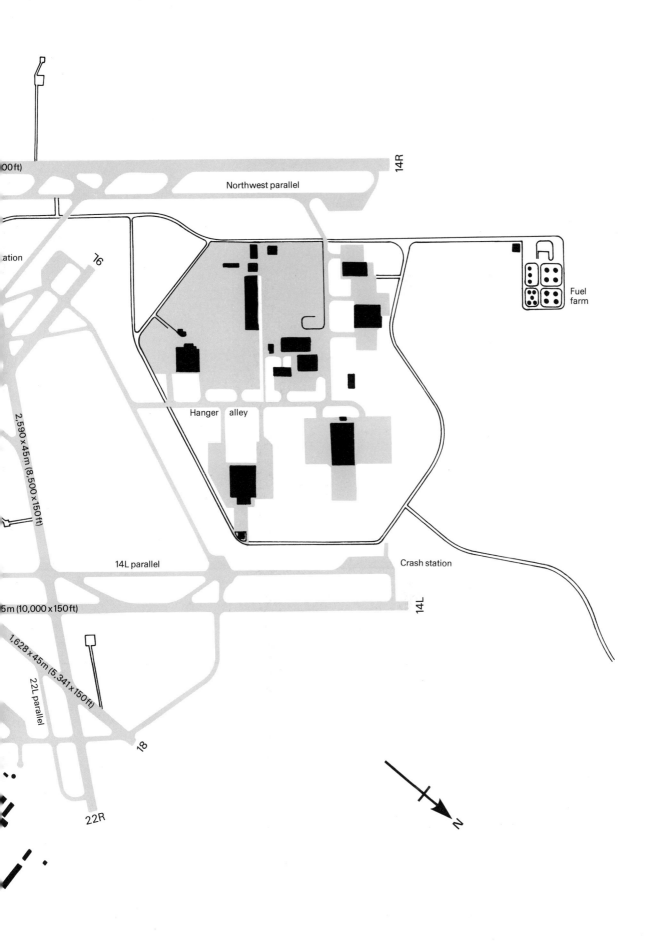

*Ground plan of Chicago O'Hare International Airport.*

00 ft)

14R

Northwest parallel

16

ation

Fuel farm

2,590 x 45m (8,500 x150 ft)

Hanger alley

14L parallel

Crash station

14L

5 m (10,000 x 150 ft)

1,628 x 45m (5,341 x150 ft)

22L parallel

18

N

22R

# Runways

An exotic new terminal building or a fleet of mobile lounges tend to attract far more attention than a new runway. This is fair enough. After all, a runway is no more than a strip of concrete on which an aircraft can land. In the early days there was often not even that and aircraft frequently landed on grass. The difference today is that aircraft weigh considerably more and they land and take off at far higher speeds than their unpressurized predecessors. A 747 weighs 373,500 kg (823,000 lb). Imagine that weight, including 400 passengers and 18 crew, touching down at around 240 km/h (150 mph) and it is easy to understand why there is more to building a runway than merely laying a strip of tarmac.

Hong Kong construction engineers used 20,000,000 tons of material, more than half of it for filling, when they reclaimed land from Kowloon Bay to build the Kai Tak runway. It cost the Government of Hong Kong over $130,000,000 initially, but when the wide-bodied jets came into service further expenditure was necessary to extend the runway to its present length of 3,390 m (11,130 ft).

Runways vary in length from one airport to another. Many airports have a very short one for light aircraft and business jets in addition to those used by the big jets. These runways may be very short indeed – Manchester Ringway has an 889 m (2,950 ft) second runway, while Milan's Linate, has one of the shortest of any international airport at 599 m (1,968 ft). However, it is more common for shorter runways to be between 5,000 and 8,000 ft. As far as maximum length is concerned there is no limit. In theory, the longer a runway is the better and safer for all who land on it, but in practice there is seldom enough space to build endless stretches of runway – except perhaps at Dallas-Fort Worth with its allocation of 73 km² (28 square miles). One of the longest runways in the world for civil transport aircraft is at John F. Kennedy at 4,440 m (14,572 ft).

The size and weight of the aircraft is a vital consideration when deciding on the length of a new runway. A 747 must have at least 1,980 m (6,500 ft) to land safely, although 2,440 m (8,000 ft) is a more realistic figure. A short runway will mean less chance of recovery for an aircraft making a difficult landing. A late touchdown, too far along a short run-

way, may mean that the pilot is not left with enough space to actually stop the aircraft. Some airports have additional hazards built in to keep the pilot on his toes. Innsbruck has mountains soaring up at each end of the runway while Nice and Singapore end in the sea. But Hong Kong probably takes the prize, with mountains surrounding the airport on one side, hotel buildings rising just below the flight path and a runway ending in Kowloon Bay.

The average width of a runway at an international airport is between 45-60 m (150–200 ft). It is unusual to find one less than 45 m (150 ft) wide and at newer airports they tend to be 60 m (200 ft). At Tokyo Narita, the existing runway and the other two projected ones are all 60 m (200 ft) wide. In the United States the tendency is more towards 45 m (150 ft) wide runways with a few exceptions such as the longest of the seven at Chicago O'Hare and the five at Los Angeles. London Heathrow is possibly unique in having three 90 m (300 ft) wide runways.

## Careful planning

When building a new runway or a completely new airport, the positioning and dimensions of the runways are vital. To assist the planners, every aircraft manufacturer produces a document of several hundred pages itemizing the characteristics and requirements of a new type of aircraft. It will tell the airport authorities how much the aircraft will weigh and at what speeds it can land and take off under different conditions. They will be able to see from this how long a runway needs to be to land safely, how much space must be allowed on taxiways for the new aircraft to turn and how much parking area must be

*Below The runway at Hong Kong's Kai Tak Airport stretching into Kowloon Bay.*
*Right Space is no problem at Sharjah, shimmering in the desert heat.*

allowed to accommodate the wing span of the aircraft. These aspects of planning require careful study since insufficient space or too tight a turning circle can create serious problems in manoeuvring large jets. A British Caledonian 707 once clipped a concrete lamp post at Schiphol while taxiing into a parking bay. Nobody was hurt but there was substantial damage to the aircraft.

Another problem airport planners have to contend with is the position of the runway in relation to the prevailing wind. The more restricted they are for space, the more difficult it will be to lay one or more runways of 3,600 m (12,000 ft) exactly where they want them. The climate and geographical location of a particular airport will dictate the overall weather pattern and the direction of the prevailing wind. Ideally, a runway should lie in line with the prevailing wind so that most of the time the aircraft will land or take off into the wind. If the runway lies at an angle to the wind there will be a cross wind, which may hamper both landing and take-off. While London Heathrow has two main runways both at an angle to the prevailing wind, which might suggest a source of complaint from pilots, it also has a shorter runway heading into the strong south-westerlies which occasionally trouble Heathrow. On the occasions when this short runway is used, its shortness is compensated for by the strength of the wind. A more limiting field is London Gatwick with a single main runway, which exercises the skill of the pilots in strong cross winds, especially those flying aircraft types which are not particularly pleasant to handle in such conditions.

The most practical layout for twin runways is to lay them parallel and this has been adopted by many of the new airports. The great advantage is that both can be used at once without either flow of traffic having to halt for the other. Of the seven runways at Chicago O'Hare, six of them run in parallel pairs.

A runway is identified by its magnetic heading on the compass. A pilot approaching Heathrow over London, heading west, would be told to land on runway 28 Left or 28 Right. However, if he were to approach the same parallel runways from the opposite direction their designation would become 10 Right and 10 Left. The use of 'right' and 'left' determines which of the 28 or 10 runways are to be used. Thus 28 Left, heading away from London to the west, would become 10 Right if approached from the opposite direction. Using Chicago O'Hare as a further example, parallel runways 14 Right and Left become 32 Left and Right respectively when approached from the opposite direction—confusing without a compass.

# Runway Lighting

A pilot may switch his landing lights on to scare birds away from the engines but these lights will be of little use in identifying the whereabouts of the runway. Every airport, except perhaps the most primitive grass strip, has some form of runway lighting. Different countries have, to a certain extent, adopted their own systems but the American system is the one most commonly used. Some international airports have very inadequate lighting by today's standards while others, such as London Heathrow, go to the other extreme of having a somewhat dazzling complex of thousands of lights.

The primary function of a runway lighting system is to guide the pilot in and indicate clearly the extremities of the landing area. In poor visibility when there is fog or heavy cloud, lighting is particularly important and airports can often brighten or dim the intensity of the lights according to conditions. Normally a pilot will land with the assistance of the Instrument Landing System (ILS), following the glide path for a well positioned touch down. The lights provide visual confirmation that he is on the correct approach. If the ILS should fail for any reason, or if there is a problem aboard the aircraft which compels the pilot to make a visual landing without the assistance of the ILS, the lighting is essential, particularly at night.

Before the runway actually begins there is a sequence of high-intensity centreline lights and crossbars to indicate the correct alignment of the aircraft for touchdown. The pilot can see from these approach lights whether his aircraft is centred correctly. These lights then give way to touchdown zone lights from the threshold of the runway and then single lights. Approach lights are mounted on stems which in turn sit on metal gantries. These vary in height to accommodate any irregularities in the terrain, ensuring that the lights themselves are always level. They are specially designed to give under pressure to limit damage to an aircraft if it catches one with its landing gear.

Down the centre of the bank of approach lights is a line of strobes, which indicate the centreline of the runway. This line is carried on by centrelights embedded in the surface of the runway itself. These are set in a solid casing to withstand the weight of a 300,000 kg (660,000 lb) aircraft landing directly on top of them. Just before the threshold of the runway there is an undershoot zone of 300 m (984 ft) marked by banks of red lights. These warn the pilot not to land too soon and miss the beginning of the runway. The very edge of the runway is marked by squat green threshold lights running across the entire width.

The initial stretch of runway and ideal touchdown area are marked by banks of touchdown lights ranged on either side of the centrelights within the limits of the edge lights. The edge lights run the entire length of the runway along both sides. They can be seen from both directions since they will apply to aircraft landing either way. This is not true of the approach and landing lights, which are switched on at the approach end of the runway.

One of the most useful pieces of lighting equipment, particularly for a pilot making a visual landing, are the Visual Approach Slope Indicators (VASIs). When the pilot guides his aircraft in for touchdown there is an optimum angle to adopt which will guarantee correct positioning on the runway. If the aircraft is too high or approaching at too shallow an angle it will land too far along the runway and risk overshooting. On the other hand, if it comes in at too steep and angle or too low it runs an equal risk of undershooting and missing the runway altogether. VASIs indicate the ideal 'slope', or angle of approach, by an ingenious system of red and white lights. They will tell the pilot if he is on the correct angle of approach and, if not, how to correct it.

Two lights are installed each side of the runway and each light is divided into two segments, white on top and red below. They are carefully angled and viewed by the pilot through slots positioned in front of each set of lights. On a correctly angled approach the pilot will see both red (far) and white (near) lights but as soon as he rises above the slope the red lights will disappear and he will see only white lights. He knows at once from this that he is too high. In the same way, he will know if he is too low if the white lights vanish and only the red lights are visible. Only at the correct angle can both red and white lights be seen clearly through the slots.

At some airports where there is a likelihood of snow there are additional lights on long stems which will stand clear of any ice or snow. A system of taxi lights show red or green across the entrances and exits to the runway. These act like traffic signals, indicating green where the pilot is to follow one taxiway and red where he is not to.

Lights have to be kept clean and well-maintained at all times. Regular checks are made to see that they are working properly and any faulty bulbs are replaced. This, in itself, can be quite an operation with nearly 30,000 lights at some of the major airports such as London Heathrow. Most international airports also have emergency power supplies that can take over within seconds of a power failure.

To the outside observer, good lighting would seem to be the most obvious requirement of any reasonably equipped airport. Despite this, two of the most common complaints pilots make about many major airports are poor navigational aids and inadequate or faulty runway lighting.

*Right A Swissair DC-9 makes its final approach. The landing lights are on tall, frangible stems designed to give way if accidentally hit. Below Approach and runway lights.*

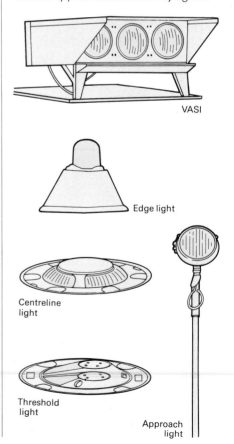

VASI

Edge light

Centreline light

Threshold light

Approach light

Edge lights (white) | Edge lights (white)
Centreline lights (white)
Touchdown zone lights (white) | Touchdown zone lights (white)
VASIs (red) | VASIs (red)
VASIs (white) | VASIs (white)
Threshold lights (green)
Approach lights (red) | Approach lights (red)
Crossbars (white)

# Air Traffic Control

Possibly the most responsible and demanding function at an international airport is the safe control of as many as 1,000 aircraft movements a day. At any given time there may be aircraft taking off or awaiting clearance for take-off on one runway while others are landing at two-minute intervals on another. If there is only one runway, landings and take-offs must be alternated on the same runway. There will be other aircraft taxiing across to join the queue for take-off and still more returning to the parking bays, while a tug may be towing yet another aircraft over to the maintenance area for inspection. In fact, the whole area – both on the ground and in the air – is alive with aircraft. A keen and constant watch must be kept to ensure that they all follow the right courses and do not pile into each other. No movement, by aircraft or ground vehicles in the movement area is allowed without instruction from the controller who monitors from the tower.

Air traffic control rooms vary in layout and design but they all retain an air of quiet calm which belies the stress under which the controllers work. The controllers must know the capabilities and characteristics of individual types of aircraft and they must make due allowance when advising pilots of their approach speeds and altitudes. Usually a lapse of two minutes, or about 6 km (4 miles), is allowed between aircraft, but a light aircraft following hot on the tail of a 747 could suffer a nasty shock if it became engulfed in the turbulence left behind by the Jumbo. On the other hand, if the 747 were following the light aircraft, the pilot of the larger aircraft might have difficulty in keeping his speed low enough to avoid running into the smaller one from behind. The air traffic controller must take all these factors into consideration when he directs aircraft movements.

Control is generally broken down into a number of stages, each handled by a separate operator who passes his aircraft on as they reach the territory of the next controller. The VHF radio frequency for the next stage is given by the controller to the pilot, and then both sign off. Both pilots and controllers are delightfully courteous even when working under pressure. There is often a polite exchange of 'good morning', when first identifying themselves, and an equally polite 'good day' when signing off. This gives a very misleading picture of the conditions under which they work, with their shared responsibility for hundreds of lives and it is not encouraged by the aviation authorities.

The geographical location of the airways control centre is often quite remote from the airport itself. For London Heathrow the airways control centre is at West Drayton, some miles from the airport complex. The airport controllers, however, occupy the airport tower where they can maintain visual contact with movements on the ground.

# Final approach

First, an aircraft approaching an airport will be guided in by an Air Traffic Control Centre (ATCC) to a holding point which may be 50 km (30 miles) or so from the airport. Depending on how much traffic is waiting to land, the aircraft may be put into a 'hold' and asked to circle a beacon along with others in the queue. They literally form an oblong spiralling stack with gaps of 300 m (1,000 ft) between each layer. Aircraft are taken off the bottom of the stack in turn and directed towards the airport. As each aircraft leaves the stack those above it each descend 300 m (1,000 ft) to take the place of the one below, the bottom one being the next to leave. If traffic is light there may be no need to hold and the pilot will be passed on to the approach controller. His job is to assist the aircraft, by use of radar, to the runway for landing. The pilot is advised at what airspeed to approach and what altitude to maintain. He is also advised to turn left or right where necessary. He will have been told which runway to use, although sometimes pilots may ask for special clearance to use a different one. This is granted to certain types of air-craft which may find it easier to land on an alternative runway. In the case of a VIP arriving who is to be deposited at a special reception point over the far side of the airport an alternative runway may also be specified.

At most airports, under normal conditions, approach for landing will be made using the Instrument Landing System (ILS). The aircraft touches down and is handed over once more, this time to the ground controller, who will have visual contact from the tower. Controllers usually identify aircraft by their call sign (flight number). One exception to this is where a non-commercial flight is concerned, and on this occasion the pilot will identify his aircraft by its registration. Thus British Airways L-1011 TriStar G-BEAM may start its working day as Speedbird 710, later become Speedbird 402 on another flight, then finally return to base empty as 'Golf Bravo Echo Alpha Mike', which is the phonetic expression of G-BEAM.

The ground controller guides the aircraft off the runway and along the taxiway, aided at some airports by a system

*All runway lighting is monitored from a central control panel situated in the tower at London Heathrow.*

of red and green taxi lights which operate like traffic signals set into the tarmac. The aircraft will follow the controller's directions into the parking bay where a marshal, or 'batsman', will be waiting to indicate the exact position for parking. At some of the more advanced airports this role has been taken over by electronic aids. The ground controller is also responsible for aircraft preparing for departure. He gives them permission to start their engines and grants the pilot's request for a 'push back' from the ramp. Aircraft have no reverse gear so a flat, heavy-duty tug is used to push them out of the parking bay on to the taxiway.

The ground controller's job is a busy one. He is not only responsible for the aircraft on the ground but for the innumerable vehicles as well, all darting about on various errands – fuel bowsers, tugs, bird scarers, 'follow me' vans, maintenance trucks, trailers and jeeps checking the runways for obstructions and patches of rubber, to name but a few. At better-equipped airports constant check on all this movement is kept on a radar screen in the tower. This shows the layout of the airport and all its taxiways and runways, registering any movement by vehicles and aircraft on the ground so that the controller does

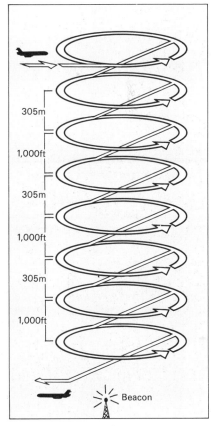

Above *Aircraft hold at intervals of 1,000 ft, circling a beacon until it is their turn to make a final approach.*

not have to rely on direct vision alone.

Air traffic control world-wide is becoming more and more complex as the number of aircraft flying at different altitudes and speeds in different directions at all times of day and night increases. The volume of traffic is constantly rising and in the last 20 years the number of passenger/km flown per year has risen from 55,000 million to a staggering 550,000 million. To cope with this situation more sophisticated equipment has gradually been developed to assist, if not actually to replace, the air traffic controllers. One advance has been the introduction of computers at some air traffic control

*Inside the control tower at Dubai International, one of the fine new Arab Emirate airports built during the last ten years.*

centres. These can provide the controller with much of the routine information essential to his job. This information is displayed in a clear and easily assimilated form, thus relieving the burden on the operator and allowing him more time to make the crucial decisions which are his primary function. The first computerized equipment was introduced in the early 1960's, and to train controllers to use the new systems, elaborate simulators have been developed. These can be programmed to create realistic situations in the same way as a flight simulator. Such installations are currently in use at various major airports, including Rome Ciampino, Amsterdam Schiphol and London Heathrow.

The operator sits in the control room and surveys the aircraft under his supervision on a circular screen. He wears a headset and microphone and communicates with the pilots by VHF radio. In the case of the latest equipment, information is fed into the console via a computer and appears displayed on the controller's screen. An aircraft is represented by a small symbol against which its code or call sign and altitude can be displayed. Some equipment can also show separately, information and essential data concerning an individual aircraft on the screen. All aircraft positions and identities can be seen at a glance, together with their altitudes, allowing the controller to make accurate decisions when directing the pilots.

Despite the cool precision with which they must work, air traffic controllers have been known to show the lighter side of their nature. A Heathrow controller has been heard to tack the latest cricket score on to his farewell to a British Airways pilot while the test match against Australia was in progress in London.

# Instrument Landing System

The instrument landing system of today is a sophisticated development of a more primitive direction-finding beacon system first used for civil aircraft after the First World War. As the progress in aircraft design necessitated higher landing speeds, more accurate aids became necessary to assist the pilot in making a safe landing. This was particularly the case in poor weather conditions and at night.

Originally the wireless operator in the aircraft would transmit on WT from a relative bearing. The ground operator would respond with the bearing and, depending on its value and its rate of change, the pilot could form a reasonably accurate picture of his position in relation to the landing field. The next system was Standard Beam Approach (SBA), which was used a great deal by the returning bombing aircraft in the last war. By this system the approach path to the runway was identified by a series of Morse signals (As and Ns). When 'on course', the transmitted sound was continuous but when to the left or right of 'course', the signal settled into either distinct As (– —) or Ns (— –). Not quite on a par with today's system but useful aids to landing in poor weather conditions all the same.

*A Boeing 737 lands as dusk falls on Munich airport. The green threshold lights are just visible across the beginning of the runway.*

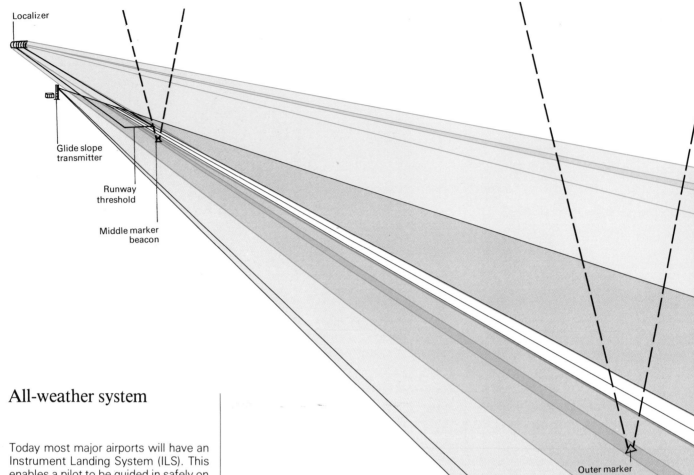

Localizer

Glide slope
transmitter

Runway
threshold

Middle marker
beacon

Outer marker
beacon

## All-weather system

Today most major airports will have an Instrument Landing System (ILS). This enables a pilot to be guided in safely on the optimum approach path for a safe landing. In good visability this is a safe and reliable system, reducing the burden of visual concentration on the pilot. In poor conditions, such as fog or bad weather, the ILS may be the only way in which a pilot has any hope of landing safely at all.

## The glide slope

The ILS consists of two transmitted signals which combine to form an invisible path along which the aircraft can approach. At the far end of the runway there is the 'localizer' beacon, which transmits a beam along a straight line of approach to the runway. At the near end of the runway, about 135 m (150 yards) from the edge, the 'glide slope transmitter' sends out a second beam in the vertical plane at an angle of 2½°–3° from the horizontal. This gives the ideal descent slope for approach.

The aircraft's position in relation to the two beams is shown on an instrument in front of the pilot. He 'establishes' the aircraft on the ILS by centralizing the aircraft along the localizer beam and descending along the glide slope. Where these two beams intersect is the ideal line and angle of approach. An aircraft 'captures' the localizer signal at about 13 km (8 miles) distance and the glide slope signal at about 600 m (2,000 ft) altitude at which stage the pilot reports at once to air traffic control.

The glide slope beam is positioned to allow a clearance of about 15 m (50 ft) from the threshold of the runway so that the point of interception is not on the very edge. This would be dangerous as it would not allow any leeway for any aircraft touching down too soon. If the aircraft follows the exact angle of the glide slope it will touch down with adequate clearance of the threshold. Problems occur when it either sinks below or rises above the optimum angle of descent. Too steep a descent will bring the aircraft down too soon, incurring the risk of undershooting and missing the beginning of the runway altogether. Too shallow an angle will extend the line of approach, bringing the aircraft down too far along the runway. On a short runway this may not allow enough distance in which to stop before ploughing off the end. A trained pilot with all instruments functioning and in adequate conditions is very unlikely to let such a thing occur, but human error can play a considerable part in causing accidents on landing.

In addition to the localizer and glide path beams there are marker beacons positioned at intervals along the approach path. The most-distant 'outer marker' is the first indication of how far the aircraft is from the runway and this marker coincides with an average approach height of about 1,500 ft. The 'middle marker' is positioned a little more than 800 m (900 yd) from the runway and, finally, the 'inner marker' sits just before the runway threshold itself, giving the pilot a good indication of where he is on the approach.

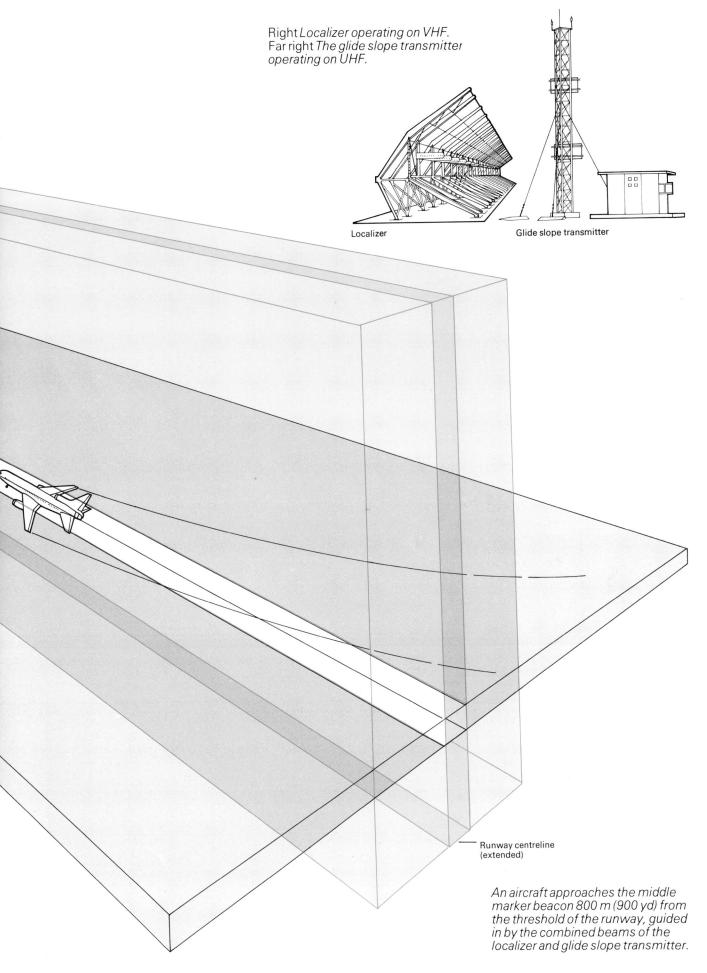

Right *Localizer operating on VHF.*
Far right *The glide slope transmitter operating on UHF.*

Localizer

Glide slope transmitter

Runway centreline
(extended)

*An aircraft approaches the middle marker beacon 800 m (900 yd) from the threshold of the runway, guided in by the combined beams of the localizer and glide slope transmitter.*

# Navigation

It is many years since a pilot had to keep glancing at a simple magnetic compass to tell him which way he was heading. As air travel itself has developed, so have the navigational aids both aboard the aircraft and on the ground. The first of these 'navaids' to be carried aboard was the direction-finding loop aerial. It rotated, picking up signals from ground stations which could be identified on a map carried by the pilot. Information from two ground stations enabled him to fix his position. By today's standards it sounds long-winded but it was a great advance on the naked eye. On today's aircraft there is no need for the pilot to make any calculations himself as it is all done automatically by far more sophisticated equipment.

The airspace above our heads is teeming with aircraft all flying off to different destinations at different altitudes. Regardless of where they are heading they must all rely on the ground to guide them at least in the initial part of their flight. However sophisticated the equipment on the flight deck, nearly all will still require some signal from the ground from which to take bearings. At present the most common ground system is the Very High Frequency Omni-directional Range (VOR) beacon. The pilot finds his way along a route by flying from one VOR beacon to the next. He knows where they are from a map of the area, which shows each beacon represented by a large compass rose with a six-sided symbol in the centre. Each one shown on the map will be identified by its station name, frequency and Morse call sign.

The VOR station itself is usually housed in a solid, pillbox structure standing on an unobstructed hill top, in open fields or on other exposed ground. Transmissions from the beacon are made on the VHF radio band between 112 MH/z and 118 MH/z. Because the pilot steers by a direction indicator synchronized with a magnetic compass, magnetic rather than true information is used. The idea of the beacon is to inform the airborne receiver of the bearing of the aircraft in relation to the ground station which sends out two signals. One signal sent out from the ground is 'omni-directional' and the other is a rotating directional signal. The airborne receiver 'listens' to both signals, compares the time lapse between receiving them and then uses this information to calculate electronically the bearing in degrees from Magnetic North. If the signals are simultaneous or 'in phase' the aircraft is positioned along the Magnetic North bearing or 'radial'. The time difference between the signals enables the aircraft's instrument to calculate along which radial the aircraft's position lies.

Aboard the aircraft itself the equipment consists of a receiver, an indicator unit and a V-shaped aerial. The receiver has an on/off switch with an identification position to bring in the three-letter Morse signal transmitted at intervals by the ground station to identify itself. The required bearing is set by the Omni-Bearing Selector (OBS) knob, which sets a compass rose on the outer rim of

*Right* Pilot's-eye view of the runway and surrounding countryside, and the predecessor to today's highly sophisticated navigation systems. *Below* A Doppler VOR beacon.

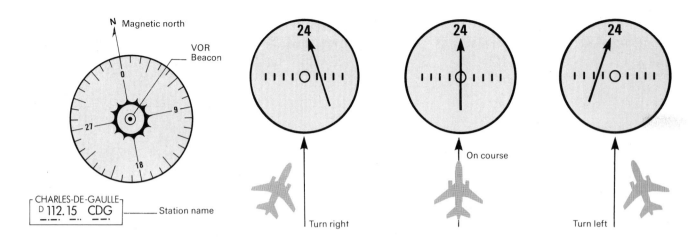

CHARLES-DE-GAULLE
D 112.15 CDG —— Station name

On course

Turn right

Turn left

Above *The location of a VOR station is represented on a chart by a compass rose and the name, call sign and frequency on which the station transmits.*

Above *The deviation indicator points to the selected radial at the top while the needle swings to left or right of the centre circle to tell the pilot whether or not he is on course.*

Below left *No need for a VOR to tell this Air Canada L-1011 TriStar pilot he is flying over Montreal.*
Below right *The eight beacons which make up the Omega system.*

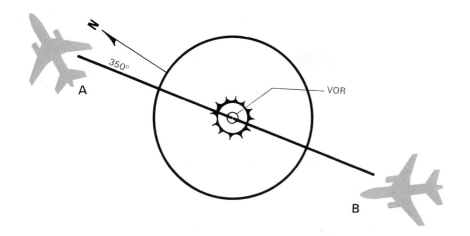

Above *The pilot knows he is on course from the position of the deviation indicator but he will also want to know on which side of the VOR he is situated. TO and FROM* flags *tell him at once the position of the aircraft in relation to the selected radial. Aircraft 'A' will receive the FROM signal, while aircraft 'B' will receive the TO signal.*

the indicator unit. The pilot looks at a vertical needle known as the deviation indicator or cross-pointer. This pivots against a dial showing whether or not the aircraft is on course. The needle, or pointer, positioned across the centre of the circle on the dial indicates that the aircraft is on course. To each side of this centre there are $2\frac{1}{2}°$ calibrations. If the pointer shifts away from the 'on course' centre to one of these calibrations, the pilot can see at once the amount by which the aircraft is deviating from its course and which way he must steer to regain the desired course.

An aircraft following a particular radial will in time reach the ground station and pass over it. If the pilot continues on the same course without resetting his VOR equipment, the instrument will tell him that he is still flying the course of the selected radial but that his position is now on the line of the radial extended

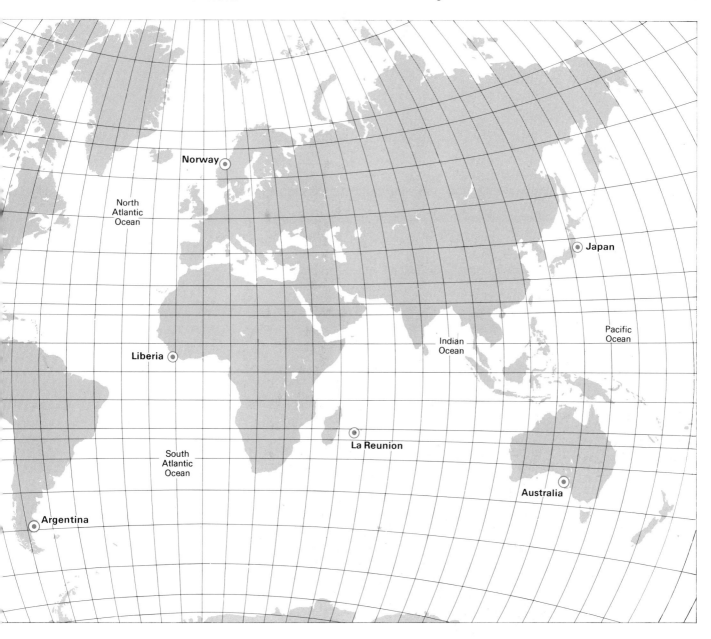

beyond the station. It tells him this by a small sign or flag on the indicator unit which changes from 'TO' to 'FROM'.

## ADF

A much older, but still used, system than the VOR is the Automatic Direction Finding (ADF). In the early days this consisted of an aerial and a radio over which the pilot and ground control struggled to be heard above the static and interference. The modern version is much improved but is still based on the same principles. The main component of the ADF is the Relative Bearing Indicator, or radio compass. This gives the pilot his 'relative bearing' by a pointer which shows where the station is in relation to the nose of the aircraft. This relative bearing is shown regardless of the aircraft's heading, and the pointer is only centred when the station is dead ahead of the aircraft.

The ADF ground station consists of a transmitter and an aerial operating between frequencies of 200 KHz and 800 KHz. The range of the signal varies according to the power of the transmitter. Climatic conditions can affect the strength and quality of the signal as well, and mountains in the vicinity can distort it. ADF is more difficult to tune than VOR and it is also subject to greater inaccuracies.

## Doppler

There is one navigation system which is entirely self-contained and can be situated either on the ground or aboard the aircraft. The Doppler is used extensively in military aircraft, which can carry the system aboard rather than rely on a ground station. The new multi-role Panavia Tornado is equipped with Doppler. The radar housed in the installation sends out three or four beams on to the ground at a specific frequency. The beams are reflected back off the ground to the aircraft overhead. By analysing the shift in frequencies of the forward and rear beams as the radar energy bounces back from the ground, the radar's computer can determine the speed and course of the aircraft while

*Having taken off, the pilot of this BAC One-Eleven will hold his course by taking bearings from a network of VOR stations.*

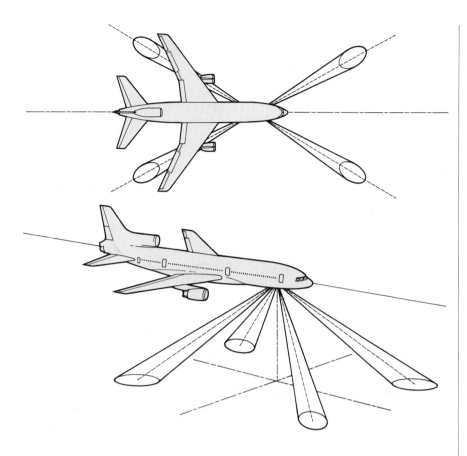

Omega system. This is relatively new and has proved to be far more accurate than other comparable systems. Eight transmitters are positioned around the world, each sending out very powerful long-range signals. These radio signals can be picked up not only by aircraft, but by ships and submarines as well, so they are multi-role. Each transmitter sends out three pulses of one second each within an interval of ten seconds, each pulse being on a separate radio frequency. The signals are synchronized and their transmission times recorded by an atomic clock. A computer aboard the aircraft receives the signals, compares and analyses them and then calculates the position of the aircraft anywhere in the world.

Progress in navigation aids will not stop with the Omega system. Already even more advanced systems are being tried out which involve lasers and satellites. The satellite navigation system should be able to determine an aircraft's position to within 10 m (33 ft).

## Inertial navigation

*Above Doppler radar determines the speed and direction of an aircraft by measuring changes in the frequency of transmitted beams reflected back from the ground.*

accommodating any drift in the signals caused by wind. The Doppler system is less commonly used by civilian transport at the present time.

Far more useful for civil aircraft is the

All the navaids mentioned so far have required radio beams or ground stations for their operation. There is one system which can be carried aboard the aircraft and which can tell the pilot with incredible accuracy what his position is with-

out any reference to outside signals of any description. The Inertial Navigation System (INS) is probably the most valuable navaid of all. It is an amazing device which makes no reference to ground stations, beacons, radio signals, lasers or satellites. Although the instrument itself is complex and highly sophisticated, the principle on which it works is very simple.

The main components consist of an inertial platform, a clock, a computer, a display unit and a control panel. There is an emergency battery to provide an auxilliary power source should the main supply fail. The inertial platform is stabilized by gyroscopes to align itself with True North, always remaining level with the earth's surface. By always aligning with True North the navigation can be worked out on the longitudinal and latitudinal lines of an ordinary atlas. Calculations made by a computer are more accurate on this basis than on that of the earth's magnetic field, which is often variable and distorted.

The stabilized platform acts as a base for two accelerometers whose pendulum-like movement can accurately measure the acceleration of the aircraft. They are set at right angles to each other – North-South and East-West when the platform is aligned with True North. The acceleration of the aircraft in the two lines of direction of the accelerometers can be measured and, by combining these readings, the computer can calculate the actual direction in which the aircraft is moving and its rate of acceleration. By integrations with time the computer can calculate the speed at which the aircraft is flying and the distance travelled. When the aircraft is no longer accelerating, the computer notes the most recent speed

Left *A closer look at a Doppler VOR situated in a field and unobstructed by buildings and rising ground.* Below *The gyroscope, a simple yet invaluable component.*

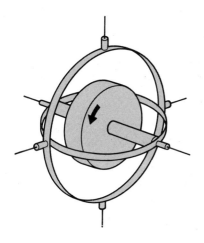

attained and assumes that it is still flying at that speed. The computer will continue to assume this until further acceleration or deceleration is recorded and thus calculate the precise distance and direction in which the aircraft has travelled from its original starting point.

All this is hidden from the pilot who looks at a display and control panel. Numbers appear in the windows on the panel, recording whatever information the pilot selects. This is often the position of the aircraft in terms of its longitude and latitude but it will also indicate windspeed, drift, groundspeed and distance and time to the next waypoint. As it proceeds along its route, so this information is updated and changes on the display. Another window displays the starting position of the aircraft and this must be fed into the system at least 15 minutes before departure. The calculations of the computer are all relative and therefore it must be told its 'position' before starting out. From that point of reference it can then calculate any

new position of the aircraft.

The system also has the capacity to record up to nine 'waypoints' at any one time. These are like mental landmarks and they help the navigation system to find its way from A to B. These waypoints can be altered and updated en route as the pilot wishes. He is kept informed all the time *from* which waypoint the aircraft is travelling and *towards* which one it is moving. As the aircraft approaches a particular waypoint a light signals a warning and the autopilot will turn the aircraft on to a new course for the next waypoint.

*An inertial navigation control panel and display unit. The numbers at the top indicate the latitude and longitude of the aircraft at any given moment. Other information can however, be selected. The pilot can select read-outs on groundspeed, direction or wind speed, for example.*

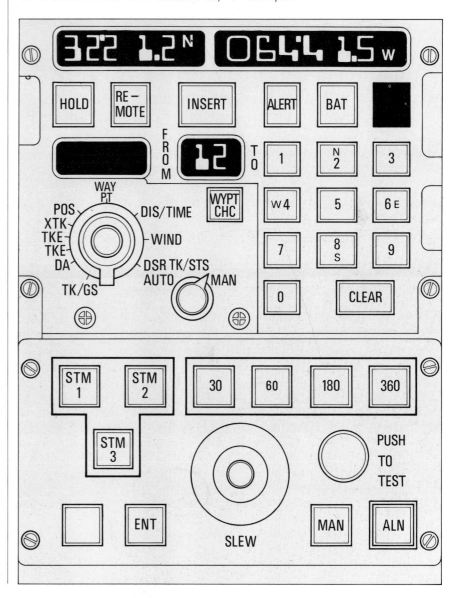

# Flight

# Flight Controls

Apart from travelling in reverse, an aircraft will fly and manoeuvre in practically any way the pilot directs it. It can gain or lose height, turn in one direction or another and pitch or roll on demand. Some aircraft are built to perform these manoeuvres to an extent which many others are not capable. The tiny aerobatic Pitts Special bi-plane is probably the most versatile aircraft ever built. It can fly upside down, perform tight rolls and turns and hair-raising stall turns. Some military trainers such as the Hawk, flown by the RAF Red Arrows display team, can perform precision manoeuvres at speeds in excess of 550 km (350 mph) in perfect formation. The Pitts and the Hawk are very different aircraft in terms of design and capability, but they both fly on the same principles, as do the civil transport aircraft used by the everyday passenger.

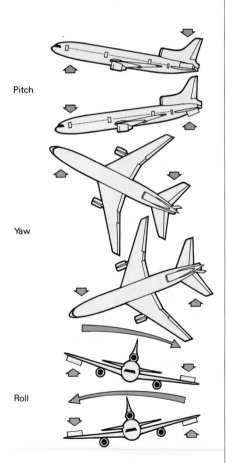

Pitch

Yaw

Roll

Right *The four opposing forces which combine to keep an aircraft in the air by each counterbalancing the other.*

## Pitch, yaw and roll

No pilot or passenger would expect Concorde or a 747 to perform a barrel roll as it pulls away from Kennedy Airport, and neither aircraft was designed to do so. But the basic principles of flight still apply. The simplest way to explain the ways in which an aircraft can move is to imagine the aircraft on a pivoted stand. The pivot represents the point of balance. Tipping the nose up and down will create 'pitch'. When an aircraft goes into a dive the nose is pitched downward; when it climbs on take-off it is pitched upward. Swivelling the nose from side to side will cause 'yaw', and rocking the aircraft from side to side by its wing tips will cause 'roll'. This can be seen when an aircraft banks around at an angle as it turns.

Each of these three manoeuvres is controlled by specific devices built into the wings and tailplane of the aircraft. Pitch is controlled by the horizontal stabilizer on the tail. The rear edges, or 'elevators,' move up or down to make the aircraft climb or dive. The yaw is controlled by the vertical stabilizer or tail-fin, the rear section of which forms the rudder. The rudder works in exactly the same way as on a boat. By moving it to left or right the pilot can make the aircraft yaw accordingly. To make the

Left *An aircraft's ability to pitch is controlled by elevators set into the horizontal stabilizer or tailplane. By deflecting them up or down the nose of the aircraft can be made to pitch up or down respectively. Yaw is controlled by the rudder, set into the vertical stabilizer or tailfin. By deflecting the rudder to the right the nose can be made to yaw to the*

aircraft roll there are two 'ailerons', one on each wing. These are used in contradiction to each other, so that one is raised when the other is lowered. When the starboard aileron is raised there is a loss of lift on that wing. At the same time, a gain in lift is achieved by lowering the corresponding aileron on the port side. This combination of lift on one side and loss of lift on the other causes the aircraft to roll.

## Control surfaces

In addition to the ailerons, which are relatively small on the newer jets, there are 'trailing edge flaps' which run the length of the rear edge of the wing between the ailerons and the fuselage. The whole front, or 'leading edge', of the wings may carry leading edge slats, which are used to achieve increased lift for landing and take-off. Ahead of the trailing edge flaps there are spoilers which assist the ailerons. When a spoiler is raised that wing drops. To turn left or right an aircraft must roll as it turns, in the same way that a motorcyclist leans over when taking a bend at speed. To turn right, the ailerons are deflected in opposite directions. The right one goes up to make the starboard

right and vice versa. Roll is achieved by alternate motion of the ailerons on the wingtips. The right wing must be raised by downward deflection of the aileron while the left wing is being lowered by upwards movement of the aileron on that side. To roll the other way the ailerons must be used in reverse.

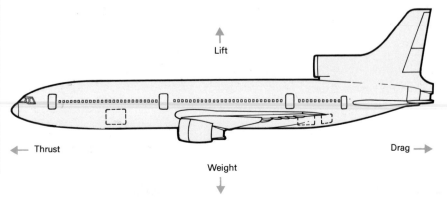

Lift

Thrust

Weight

Drag

wing tilt downwards, while the left aileron goes down to make the port wing tilt up. The elevator is tilted upwards very slightly to stabilize the aircraft as it turns. The rudder is not used actually to turn the aircraft but to prevent it yawing from side to side and to oppose, for example, the yaw caused by an engine failure.

## Delta wing

These complicated arrangements of flaps, slats, spoilers and ailerons apply only to conventional subsonic aircraft. Supersonic delta-wing aircraft, such as Concorde and the Tupolev TU-144, are completely streamlined to achieve the minimum of drag necessary to cruise at twice the speed of sound. This means a minimum of external devices, and so those that do exist must perform more than one function. There are no leading edge slats on Concorde and, since there is no horizontal stabilizer on the tail, there are no elevators. Instead there are combined elevator/ailerons on the trailing edges of the wings called 'elevons'. There are three elevons on each side of the wing trailing edge. They all work together to provide pitch, and the left and right sets work opposingly to provide roll. Trim is maintained from within

the aircraft by the transfer of fuel to and from the front and rear trim tanks, altering the centre of gravity accordingly.

The pilot controls the movement of an aircraft by co-ordinating his use of the control column and two large pedals at his feet. The elevators are operated by pushing or pulling on the column – for-

ward to drop the nose and backwards to lift it. By turning a wheel mounted on the column to left or right the pilot can operate the ailerons, causing the aircraft to roll to left or right respectively. The rudder is operated by pressing either the left or the right foot pedal, according to which direction the pilot chooses.

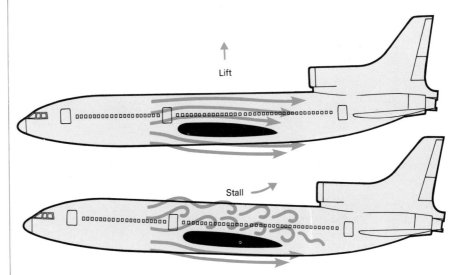

Above *When climbing, the increased angle at which the wing meets the airstream causes an increase in lift. As the camber of the top surface is greater than that of the underside of the wing, the upper flow of air is* *forced to travel further, increasing the downward acceleration of the airflow. Wing stall occurs when this angle becomes too great. The airflow becomes turbulent, resulting in a critical loss of lift.*

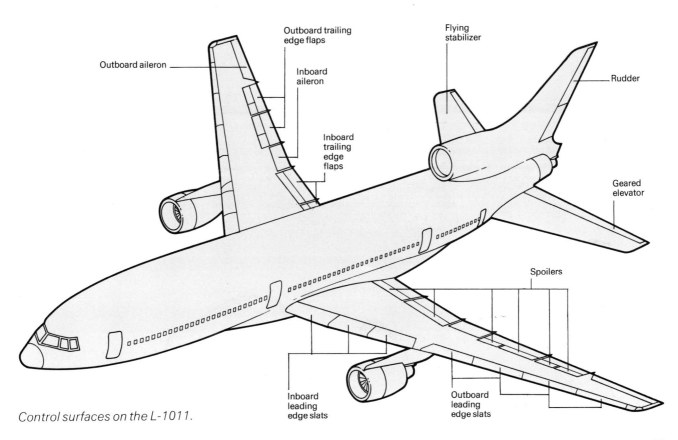

*Control surfaces on the L-1011.*

# Take-off

There are certain preparations that must be made and preliminary paperwork to be dealt with before an aircraft can leave the ground. The flight itself will have been scheduled months in advance and details of it and all the other flights available from that airline sent to booking agents around the world.

The flight has been booked, the tickets issued and the passengers are boarding. The flight crew will have split up and gone about their separate tasks. The flight engineer must supervise the refuelling and last minute checks on the aircraft and verify that all systems aboard are working properly. This includes everything from cabin lighting to the engines. Meanwhile the captain

and his co-pilot (first officer) are being briefed for the flight by Flight Dispatch. Briefing can take between a quarter of an hour and half an hour depending on the length of the flight and the conditions that day. The captain is given the latest information on weather conditions on his route and told what to expect in the way of rain, snow, thunderstorms and difficult winds and turbulence. A weather chart will be prepared in advance showing which routes are available and which are the best for his particular journey.

The captain chooses his route and then receives the full details of the flight he is about to make, usually from a computer. The computer will tell him

everything he needs to know to get to his destination. In case of difficulties or adverse weather conditions he will also check out alternative airports at which he can land if necessary. Having decided all this, he then has to register his flight plan and confirm his proposed route with air traffic control. They will pass on the information to the various control centres along the route, including that of the final destination point.

The captain and first officer now take their seats on the flight deck with the flight engineer, who has already arrived. There is a standard routine of pre-take-off checks which must be made before the aircraft can leave the ground. Instruments are checked, controls

positioned correctly and all the emergency warning systems are tried out to be sure they are functioning. When the captain is confident that the aircraft is ready to fly and he has been told that all the passengers are aboard and strapped in, the flight can depart.

## Starting up

An external power unit is used to start the engines and the captain requests a 'push back', in other words, assistance to leave the parking bay. A heavy-duty tug is used to push the aircraft on to the taxiway. As all ground movement including airport vehicles in the aircraft movement areas comes under the control of traffic control the pilot must ask the controller for permission for his push back.

Once out of the parking bay, the con-troller will tell the pilot to follow a par-ticular taxiway for take-off on whichever runway is in use. While aircraft are within sight on the ground the controller refers to them when addressing other aircraft by type and airline to avoid con-fusion. There is no point in telling the captain of a Pan Am 747 to follow flight BA 174. He may know that means a British Airways flight but there may be several British Airways aircraft ahead of him and he will not know the flight num-bers. He will be told by the controller to queue for take-off behind the British Airways TriStar or the Qantas 747, poss-ibly quoting the last two letters or digits of their registrations as well. When his turn comes, the captain manoeuvres the aircraft into position on the runway and waits for clearance from control.

The Boeing 747 is an excellent aircraft to serve as a model for explaining take-off procedures. All the time he has been waiting, the captain of the 747 has been making mental checks to confirm that all is in order. He will also have considered what to do in the case of a possible abort. If he has to abandon the take-off at the last minute, he will have no time to stop and check the runway condi-tions, to see which way the wind is blowing or to decide how to control 360,000 kg (800,000 lb) of aircraft.

## Take-off

Finally, the moment of take-off has arrived. The throttles are pushed for-ward and the aircraft gains speed. As the 747 approaches its take-off speed of about 290 km/h (180 mph) the captain reaches his 'decision speed'. This is the point at which he must decide once and for all whether to take off or abort. This point is known as $V_1$ (Velocity One). Every second the aircraft accelerates forward there is less and less runway on which the aircraft can stop, so the pilot has no time to waste. Once he has decided to go ahead with the take-off and passes $V_1$ he must forget all thoughts of aborting in an emergency. His priority from then on is to keep the aircraft in the air.

The actual speed for initiating take-off is known as $V_R$ (Velocity-rotate). The control column is pulled back and the nose of the 747 lifts or 'rotates' into the air at an angle of about 12°. When the aircraft is positively airborne the landing gear is retracted to reduce drag. Gradu-ally the flaps, which have been extended for take-off, are retracted as the 747 gains height and speed and the aircraft climbs away to find its cruise altitude. This may not be possible at once if the surrounding airspace is con-gested. The aircraft may have to attain its desired altitude in stages, as space becomes available. The cruise speed of the 747 is around 890 km/h (550 mph). It has four engines, manufactured by Pratt & Whitney of the United States or by Rolls-Royce of the United Kingdom, depending on the airline operating. Between them the engines develop some 100,000 kg (220,000 lb) thrust on take off.

Once the aircraft settles in its climb the pilot can engage the autopilot and think about welcoming his passengers aboard. The 'no smoking' signs go out and, unless there is severe turbulence, the 'fasten seat belts' lights will go off as well. However, this is assuming that the take-off was without incident. What happens if an engine fails just before the speed reaches $V_1$? The pilot must act quickly and calmly, without wasting a second of valuable time or a fraction of runway. First he shuts all power off and begins braking, very hard at first, keep-ing the aircraft straight on the runway. This is particularly important. He raises the spoilers and reverses thrust to act as a further brake on the aircraft's speed. The wheel brakes are not enough to stop a 360,000 kg (800,000 lb) aircraft travelling at 240 km/h (150 mph) so the engines must share the load.

The $V_1$ speed is calculated to allow enough runway for an aircraft to stop in an emergency. This speed varies according to the aircraft type. If the pilot has carried out his take-off in the correct manner and made his decision to abort at the right moment, he should have no trouble in stopping by the end of the runway. If, on the other hand, the pilot has passed $V_1$ and is on the point of becoming airborne when an engine fails, he must go on. Today's jets are designed to take off with one engine failed and an engine failure does not therefore mean that the aircraft is lost. Once safely off the ground the pilot would probably circle the airport and request permission to land as soon as possible to inspect the damage.

It is not uncommon to see an aircraft abort a landing or a take-off at an inter-national airport. Often the cause is nothing as dramatic as an engine failure. A suspected fault in the landing gear or the hydraulic system generally may require a visual inspection from the tower for safety's sake. If everything looks satisfactory, the tower will give the all clear, but the pilot will be particu-larly attentive when he lands at his des-tination in case a fault does develop.

*A Boeing 747 takes off from Kai Tak, Hong Kong's international airport on the shore of Kowloon Bay.*

# Landing

In the comfort of today's jet aircraft it is very easy to forget that you are flying at all. The flight may have lasted 17 hours during which time much of the actual flying will have been controlled by the autopilot. However, once the aircraft approaches its destination, the pilot must be ready to resume full control for landing. This does not imply that he has wandered off during the flight and put his feet up. Far from it! But his role changes from one of supervising and monitoring systems which are controlled by an electronic brain to one of direct control by his own hand.

## Holding point

Landing requires even more thought and judgement than take-off. The pilot must consider any reasons for not making the landing and must also be clear in his mind what he will do if he is forced to abort at the last minute. On a normal flight he will be guided in by a series of radio beacons or VOR (Very High Frequency Omnidirectional Radio Range) situated on the ground at intervals along the flight path. Air traffic control will ask the pilot to inform them when he reaches a 'holding point' where the aircraft will probably be stacked until its turn comes to land. Busy airports are sometimes forced to ask aircraft to hold for as long as an hour before landing. The aircraft fly in a spiral, one on top of the other at intervals of 300 m (1,000 ft), gradually descending lower and lower in the stack until they reach the lowest level. Once at the bottom, it is that aircraft's turn to leave the stack and make the final approach.

## QFE vs QNH

The traffic controller will ask the pilot to report his speed and height. He will then tell him whether he should turn left or right and what speed and altitude to adopt. At this point the pilot will also be advised of the altimeter settings for landing. This refers to the barometric pressure at the airport and the elevation of the runway that he will be using. An altimeter works on the barometric pressure at the altitude at which the aircraft is flying. It is important that the pilot should know what the barometric pressure is on the ground before he lands and, of course, the elevation of the airport above or below sea level. With these two pieces of information he can then set the barometric pressure subscale on his altimeter (the device which compensates for day-to-day changes in atmospheric pressure) so that, depending on his choice of two philosophies, the instrument will either read zero or the height of the runway above sea level at the moment of touchdown. The world's airline pilots are rather split over this choice. Those who prefer to see zero feet at touch down (the QFE party) laud its simplicity; those who prefer runway elevation (the QNH party) like the height-of-terrain awareness that the latter invokes.

The next task is to locate and establish the aircraft on the Instrument Landing System (ILS). These invisible radio beams will guide the aircraft in via the instruments on the flight deck. Civil aircraft operations work in reverse to military ones, where the instruments are on the ground and the aircraft merely reflects a radar beam. The ground controllers guide the fighter in from below whereas on a civil aircraft the pilot guides the aircraft in, using the instrumentation aboard. One reasoning for this is that in a military aircraft it will always be your own air force doing the controlling but in a civil aircraft you don't know who is in charge on the ground, so the airlines are happier relying on their

*An El Al 747 with its landing gear down seconds before touchdown.*

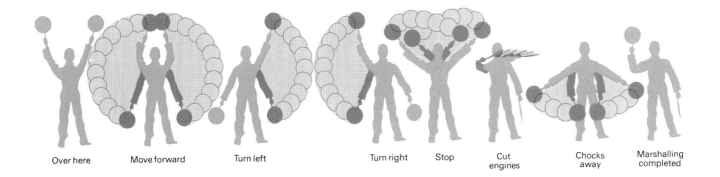

Over here    Move forward    Turn left    Turn right    Stop    Cut engines    Chocks away    Marshalling completed

*Signals used by marshals, or batsmen, when guiding an arriving aircraft into a parking bay.*

own chosen pilots.

Once established on the ILS, the next point of reference will be the 'outer marker'. This is a beacon located just outside the airport perimeter and is the last point of reference before the pilot sees the runway approach lights.

*Controller:* 'Clipper One, you are two miles from the outer marker, cleared for ILS approach, runway 28 Left.'

*Pilot:* 'Clipper One, cleared for ILS runway 28 Left.'

Every piece of information or instruction is confirmed back to be sure that it has been correctly interpreted. After a short delay the aircraft will actually pass over the outer marker.

*Pilot:* 'Clipper One, outer marker inbound.'

*Controller:* 'Thank you Clipper One, you are cleared to land runway 28 Left, wind is 330 at 2. Call tower on 118.5. Good day.'

*Pilot:* 'Clipper One, cleared to land 28 Left, tower on 118.5. Good day.'

The number of times the pilot has to change radio frequencies depends on the size of the airport and how busy it is. It can often require three or four different stages of control. English tends to be the international language of traffic control although some airports have better reputations than others for being comprehensible over the air. One thing both pilots and controllers do have is a reputation for being extremely polite to each other.

The pilot now makes his final approach. The landing gear is down, the passengers are all seated and everyone is strapped in. The flaps are lowered at about 1,500 ft and the aircraft begins to descend, guided in by the ILS as it gradually loses height. The touchdown point indicated by the ILS is not on the very threshold of the runway but 300 m (1,000 ft) along it to avoid any danger of undershooting. If the pilot allows the aircraft to sink below the glide path he will miss the ideal touchdown point and land too soon. If he lets the aircraft rise

above the glide path he will land too far along the runway and may not have enough space to stop before overshooting.

A 747 lands at about 240 km/h (150 mph). The pilot brakes and the spoilers are raised. The engine thrust is reversed and this is maintained at progressively lower powers until the aircraft has slowed to taxiing speed. Traffic control will then direct the aircraft off the runway and into a parking bay.

In the event of some problem developing, the pilot still has a last-minute option to 'go around'. He increases the engine thrust to its maximum and 'rotates' the aircraft. In other words, he pulls up the nose of the aircraft to climb away from the runway. From then onwards the procedure is very similar to a normal take-off. Once safely airborne again, the pilot can decide how to tackle the problem and inform control of any malfunction or potential danger. Faulty landing gear might require a foam landing, in which case the aircraft can circle while the emergency services are alerted.

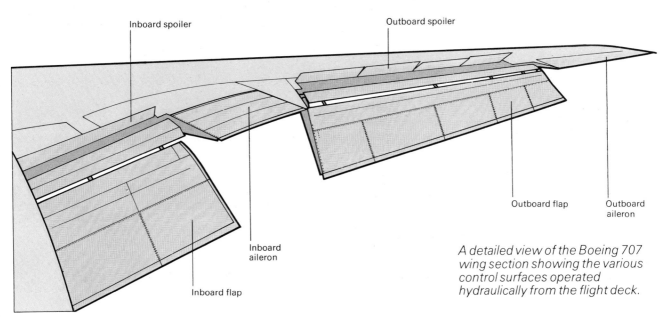

Inboard spoiler    Outboard spoiler    Outboard flap    Outboard aileron    Inboard aileron    Inboard flap

*A detailed view of the Boeing 707 wing section showing the various control surfaces operated hydraulically from the flight deck.*

A Southern Airways DC-9 en route to Atlanta attempted an emergency landing on State Spur Highway 92 in Georgia after losing power in both its engines in severe weather conditions. Of the 85 passengers aboard about 62 were killed and the aircraft destroyed. On another occasion, a HS125 business jet was approaching Luton, England at about 2,200 ft in heavy cloud, snow and sleet. The landing gear was down and the airspeed about 270 km/h (170 mph) as the aircraft established on the ILS. Suddenly a streak of lightning struck the nose, causing a large flash and a bang. The right-hand windscreen shattered and the ILS indicator packed up, although the radar and other aids continued to function. The aircraft managed to land without injury to the crew but the nose-cone had become completely detatched from the fuselage. It was found some distance away, lying on the ground. There had been no report of thunderstorms prior to landing.

Landing and take-off are considered to be the most likely occasions for an incident to occur, and recent thinking confirms that the approach and landing are the most hazardous. The various official bodies concerned with aircraft safety consider one fatal accident for every 2,000,000 flights bearable and on the whole the industry does keep within this figure. Overall, the statistics reflect nothing but credit on the aircraft manufacturers, the airlines and the pilots.

Safe landings depend on safe conditions on the ground. Runways must therefore be kept clear at all times. Ice, snow, water, debris and patches of rubber are all potential hazards. One of the greatest dangers of landing on a wet runway is aquaplaning. This is when the tyres fail to grip the surface of the runway and merely ski across the surface of the water not unlike driving on a rain-soaked highway. Special textured surfaces have been developed with grooves in the concrete to provide maximum adhesion under slippery conditions. To cope with snow there are vehicles with enormous rotating brushes as well as snow ploughs to clear snow and slush. Heating a runway is very costly although some airports have tried to do this to cope with ice and snow. A far cheaper method is to use anti-icing fluid spread over the surface of the runway to disperse the ice. Brushers clean off any rubber left by aircraft tyres, and magnetic vacuum cleaners suck up any nuts, bolts or other bits of stray metal on the runway — the origins of which most passengers would probably prefer not to know.

*A McDonnell Douglas DC-10 Series 30 coming in to land.*

# Automatic Landing

Most major airports today have an ILS but only about one in four world-wide is equipped with one suitable for autoland. Of these airports, only a handful have equipment capable of landing an aircraft in very low visibility while still maintaining a failure rate of less than one in 10,000,000. In addition to the necessary ground installations, the aircraft using the system must be fitted with the appropriate instrumentation to be able to make a completely automatic landing without pilot aid.

The first aircraft to be fully equipped with autoland capability was the Hawker Siddeley Trident. Many millions were spent over a period of years to develop and perfect the system, which proved to be highly successful. The first fully automatic landing was made in 1972 by a Trident 3 at London Heathrow in weather conditions that would have made landing by any other means virtually impossible. The system was developed in co-operation with Smiths Industries, who supply the autopilot equipment for the Trident.

On a conventional approach, the pilot uses the autopilot to guide the aircraft in on the glide path to 200 ft. At this point the pilot takes over and lands the aircraft manually. One of the problems, particularly in poor visibility, is the small amount of time the pilot has at this crucial height. He must look up, re-focus his sight from the instrument panel in front of him to the runway ahead, then assess his position in relation to the

*Trident making an automatic landing in very poor visibility.*

runway and decide what corrective manoeuvres are necessary to achieve correct alignment. All the while the aircraft is travelling at over 240 km/h (150 mph) and losing height steadily, so that the pilot has only 22 seconds in which to make a decision regarding the flight path of the aircraft and to act on this decision before he touches down. Once down, it is too late to reposition, and if the aircraft is not in the right place it may not land on the runway at all.

TOUCHDOWN.
Pitch and Roll channels of autopilot disconnected Automatic Ground roll control down to 80 knots at which speed rudder control automatically disconnected. Ground roll monitoring provided by Ground Speed and distance-to-go indicator.

12.5 FEET.
Drift 'kick off' automatically initiated by radio altimeters.

80 KNOTS.
Automatic disengagement of rudder control. Below 80 knots PVD head-up guidance to give steering information down to taxying speed.

Taxying speed

The principle of completely automatic landing is to feed the localizer and glide slope beams into the autopilot which establishes the aircraft on the ILS. The final approach speed is controlled by an auto-throttle sub-system. The actual installation works in triplicate, with three systems working in parallel, each compared with the others. Any discrepancy between the three is noticed at once and the risk of failure reduced accordingly. Disengagement of one channel activates a warning signal to the pilot on the flight deck, but the system continues to operate. If a second chan-

nel should also disengage, the autopilot is then disconnected automatically and the pilot is obliged to take over.

With three installations doing the same job however, this happens very rarely. A system which boasts being able to land an aircraft safely while the pilot looks on had to be proved extremely reliable before it was acceptable to any certification authority. With the Smiths system the pilot's role

is essentially one of monitoring. He checks the radio altimeters, selects the 'land' mode and continues to monitor the flight path of the aircraft and the state of the automatics. At 65 ft the throttles are automatically closed and flare out begins. The nose tips up and the aircraft settles down on to the runway. Speed is reduced to 150 km/h (90 mph) and rudder control automatically disconnected. Speed and distance are monitored as the aircraft slows to taxiing speed. The pilot then takes over the controls to taxi off the runway after literally making a 'no hands' landing.

It is unfortunate that the high cost of installing this system has inhibited its use up until now. Even if the airports have the facilities to use it, not all the aircraft do. It has proved very reliable and an invaluable asset to airports located in areas plagued by fog and bad weather conditions.

Left *The spacious flight deck of a Trident fitted with autoland. The system is not used nearly as much as it deserves, mainly due to cost.* Below *Autoland requires not only the fitting of flight deck equipment but also a first class ILS with which to operate. Not every ILS is suitable to be used for autoland and many airports have found the cost too high.*

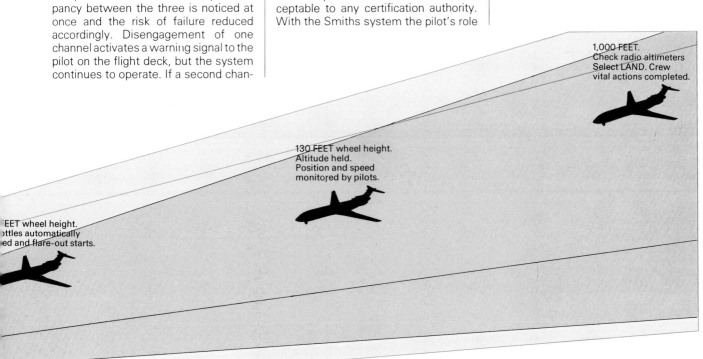

1,000 FEET.
Check radio altimeters
Select LAND. Crew
vital actions completed.

130 FEET wheel height.
Altitude held.
Position and speed
monitored by pilots.

FEET wheel height.
ottles automatically
ed and flare-out starts.

# Flight Deck

The days when a pilot flew by a combination of instinct, the sound and feel of the aircraft and what he could see in front of him are long gone. In the early days he had a magnetic compass and little else to give him a sense of direction. The flight deck has come a long way since then and today even light aircraft are often fitted with sophisticated instrumentation and flying aids. In some of the more advanced civil aircraft even the conventional instruments are being augmented by digital 'head up' displays which relay all the necessary information at a glance. This equipment is far from being standard on all aircraft yet, but it is sure to become so in the near future. It has been developed and used successfully on military aircraft for some time and is now being modified for use on civil aircraft. Instead of consulting his instruments, the pilot stares straight at the windshield, where a picture of the runway is projected in front of him. Also visible is a digital display giving the heading, speed and altitude. As the real runway approaches in his field of vision, the pilot can see it merge with the projected image on the screen. Using this as his guide with the information he requires displayed alongside it, the pilot can land the aircraft without taking his eyes off the runway. The time-saving factor may be only a few seconds, but that in itself can be crucial when landing a big jet.

Unlike driving a car, flying an aircraft requires a long list of checks to be made before the pilot can start the engines for take-off. The flight engineer will have arrived in advance to make preliminary checks before the captain and co-pilot take their seats. By tradition the captain sits on the left with his co-pilot on his right. Together they go through a long checklist of all the controls and instruments, ensuring that each one is functioning correctly. Warning systems are also checked – lights flash, alarms sound and the control stick shakes nervously to indicate stall danger. There is a warning system on the main instrument panel made up of red or amber squares which light up, accompanied by an alarm buzzer. Should any part of the aircraft or its controls fail, these warnings are activated at once. Both pilot and co-pilot each have a duplicate set of instruments so that either can take full control in the event of the other becoming incapacitated. The flight deck is carefully designed to allow the pilot to see all the instruments and reach all the controls without moving from his seat. In fact, he spends the best part of his working life sitting in that seat.

## In the pilot's seat

Flight decks can vary from aircraft to aircraft, so it is simpler to refer throughout to one particular model. The Boeing 747 is a good choice as it is not only an aircraft familiar to most members of the public but also highly regarded by the majority of pilots. The flight deck is positioned high on the top of the fuselage to allow for an upwards-opening nose door on cargo versions of the aircraft. This high position can impose certain restrictions on the pilot's field of vision but otherwise the deck is a good example of well-thought-out design. There are nine electronic audible warning 'tones' which issue from one outlet, so the pilot has to make sure he is familiar with them before he flies. Work is in progress to simplify warning systems and generally to make them more easily identifiable. The immediate impression when first viewing the flight deck of the 747 is one of clear, orderly layout and good accessibility to all the controls and instrumentation. The pilots sit at individual 'stations' while the flight engineer sits behind the co-pilot on the right facing a huge array of instruments, knobs and lever switches from which he can monitor all systems aboard the aircraft including the engine performance.

Directly in front of the pilot is the control column. This has changed little in appearance over the years. By pulling or pushing it he can lower or raise the elevators, situated on the horizontal stabilizer on the tail of the aircraft, causing it to climb or dive. Mounted on the column is a wheel which deflects the ailerons and causes the aircraft to bank and turn. At his feet the pilot has two pedals to control the rudder. This is the upright, moveable section of the tail, or vertical stabilizer, which controls the direction of the aircraft in rather the same way as on a boat. Between the two pilot's seats is a row of levers numbered 1–4. These are moulded so that they can be gripped in one hand and eased backwards or forwards to control the engine thrust. Below the thrust levers are four smaller levers, also numbered 1–4 for controlling the fuel supply. Switches on aircraft are generally 'off' when in the downward position, and 'on' when in the upward position.

To the left of this central console are sliding levers to control the stabilizer trim and the parking brakes, while on the opposite side a lever controls the flaps. On a flat, central console at the

*Horizontal situation indicator, the aircraft's main compass indicator.*

*Attitude director instrument, usually placed above the HSI on the 747.*

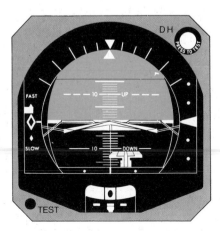

Right *Flight engineer at his station on the flight deck of a 747.*
Insets clockwise *Typical display of symbology on a Smiths Industries electronic head-up display system; primary engine instruments for the Boeing 747; throttle and engine start levers for the four-engined 747.*

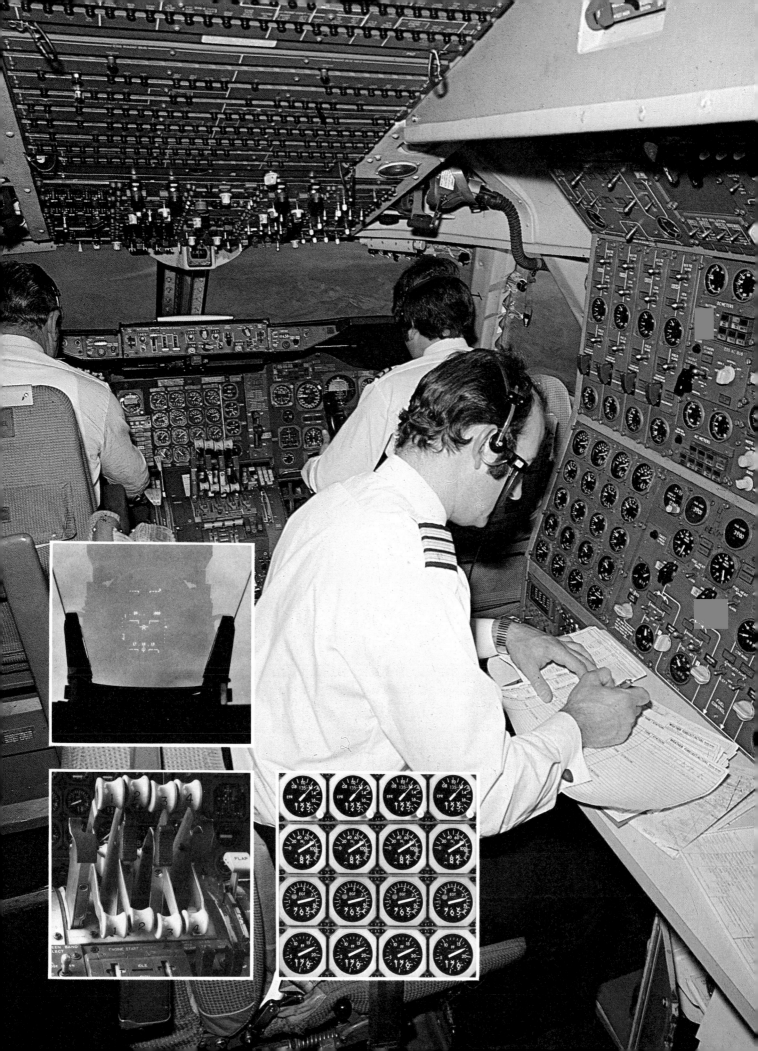

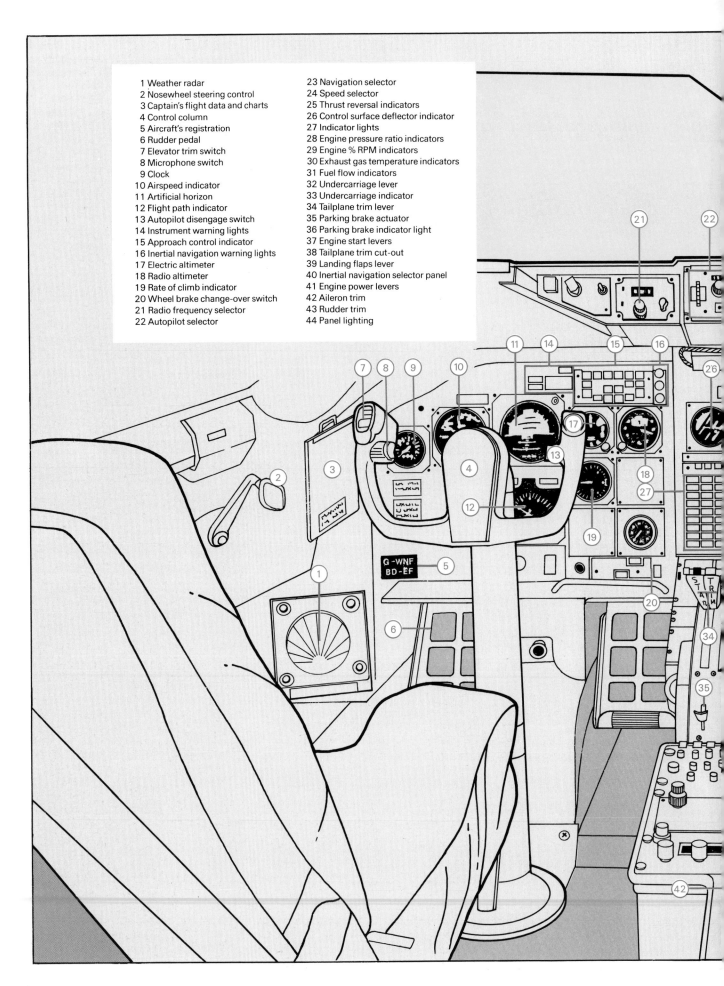

1 Weather radar
2 Nosewheel steering control
3 Captain's flight data and charts
4 Control column
5 Aircraft's registration
6 Rudder pedal
7 Elevator trim switch
8 Microphone switch
9 Clock
10 Airspeed indicator
11 Artificial horizon
12 Flight path indicator
13 Autopilot disengage switch
14 Instrument warning lights
15 Approach control indicator
16 Inertial navigation warning lights
17 Electric altimeter
18 Radio altimeter
19 Rate of climb indicator
20 Wheel brake change-over switch
21 Radio frequency selector
22 Autopilot selector
23 Navigation selector
24 Speed selector
25 Thrust reversal indicators
26 Control surface deflector indicator
27 Indicator lights
28 Engine pressure ratio indicators
29 Engine % RPM indicators
30 Exhaust gas temperature indicators
31 Fuel flow indicators
32 Undercarriage lever
33 Undercarriage indicator
34 Tailplane trim lever
35 Parking brake actuator
36 Parking brake indicator light
37 Engine start levers
38 Tailplane trim cut-out
39 Landing flaps lever
40 Inertial navigation selector panel
41 Engine power levers
42 Aileron trim
43 Rudder trim
44 Panel lighting

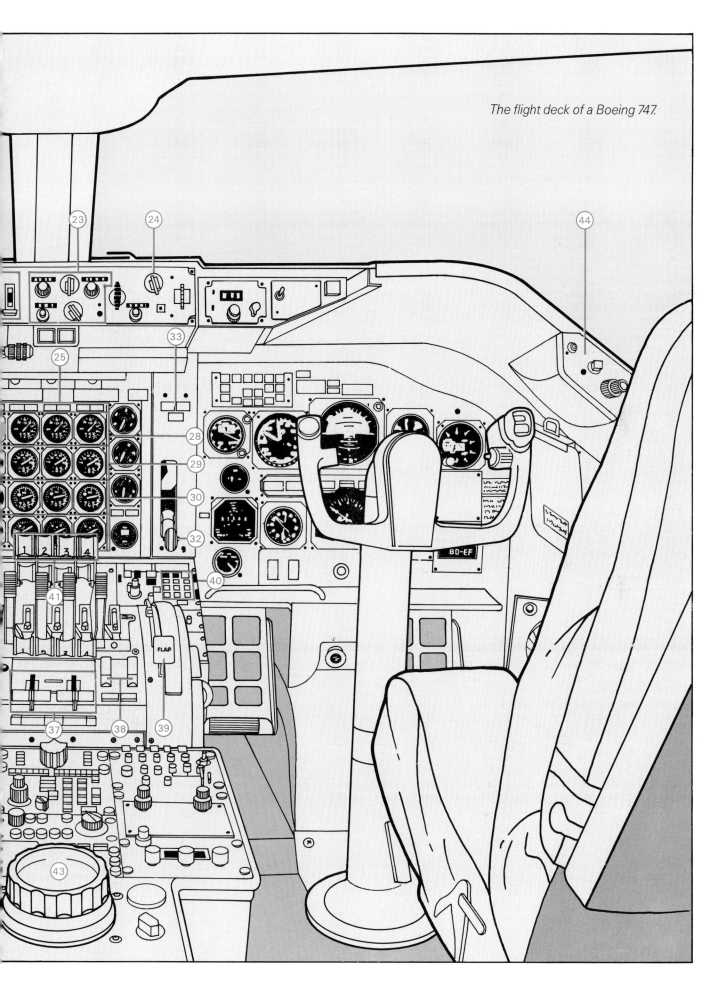

*The flight deck of a Boeing 747.*

pilot's elbow are various controls for weather radar, radio, aileron and rudder trim and the Automatic Direction Finder (ADF). In front of the pilot in the top right-hand corner are warning lights for the Inertial Navigation System (INS) and above that the navigational radio selector. To the right is the switch for engaging the autopilot. A pilot will choose whether to use this during flight or to fly manually, according to conditions. When approaching to land, he will switch it off on final approach and use the Instrument Landing System (ILS) based at the airport to guide him, or use an autolanding system if the airport has a high-quality ILS. Some large airports have this system, although many have decided against it because of the costs involved in installing and operating it.

Flight decks are not identical, even on one specific type of aircraft. The airline buying the aircraft has a say in what it actually requires when buying new. On some 747s the engine instrumentation is made up of some 20 circular dials of conventional appearance. On others, the same instrument function is carried out by 'vertical tapes' – a row of long calibrated strips with indicators, positioned above the thrust controls.

The pilots look out through a divided windshield of special toughened and laminated glass. There are side windows on each side, but these are fixed in a closed position on the 747. On some aircraft these windows can be opened and are considered to be an extra safety measure in the event of the main windshield becoming obscured. To protect the windshield from reflection there is a sculptured cowling, or 'glare shield', carefully shaped to give maximum visibility without obstruction.

Directly under the glare shield, in the pilot's main field of vision, is a group of instruments which tell him at a glance what the aircraft is doing; at what altitude, in which direction, at what speed and at what angle it is flying. There is a large and rather colourful instrument positioned directly in front of him called the 'attitude director'. The top half of the circular instrument-face is bright blue to represent sky and the lower half is brown to represent the ground. The two halves are divided by a white line to represent the horizon. A horizontal symbol is superimposed and independently mounted on the artificial horizon to represent the aircraft. The attitude director works very logically. The 'aircraft' remains fixed in position while the artificial horizon swivels to show the precise attitude, or angle, of the aircraft in relation to the ground. A computer correlates all the information displayed on the other instruments and indicates what attitude the pilot should adopt by means of pointers superim-

posed on the artificial horizon. When these are not lined-up the pilot can see at once which way to manoeuvre the aircraft to regain the correct heading.

Below the attitude director is the Horizontal Situation Indicator (HSI). This is a comprehensive guide-at-a-glance. It shows where the aircraft should be going, marked by a white square, or 'heading marker', in relation to a compass and a course arrow which indicates the actual direction of travel. Among other things, it also shows the distance from a particular station in nautical miles, and time-to-station and ground-speed or time elapsed according to what the pilot selects on the panel

below. Another important instrument for the pilot's reference is the Mach, and airspeed, indicator. This tells him both his airspeed in knots (nautical miles per hour) and the Mach number, or speed of the aircraft in relation to the local speed of sound, at any altitude. There is, of course, also an altimeter, which tells him how high he is flying. It is interesting to compare the flight deck of a 747 or any other modern subsonic jet aircraft with that of Concorde. Although Concorde can fly at twice the speed of sound it uses instrumentation similar to that found in a conventional subsonic aircraft and the layout employed is fairly standard to other civil aircraft.

A first glance at this myriad of instruments, knobs, levers and switches would leave even the most technically-minded observer completely baffled. The first impression when visiting the flight deck of an aircraft such as the 747 is to wonder how any pilot, however experienced, could possibly take in even a fraction of the information displayed. The simple answer is that he can't – and he does not attempt to. He scans all the relevant instruments at intervals, knowing exactly what to look for, but he does not sit studying one in particular for minutes at a time. There has always been an interesting argument between qualified pilots and laymen as to whether an untrained person could actually land a big jet successfully in an emergency. The pilots said 'no'; the theorists said 'yes'. To answer the question once and for all, BBC radio decided to put it to the test. A volunteer who had never flown an aircraft of any description took the pilot's seat in a similator to enact an 'emergency' situation where the pilot had suddenly dropped down dead of a heart attack in mid-flight. From the 'ground' a pilot and a traffic controller guided the aircraft in to land, control by control, step by step. They told the volunteer pilot exactly what to do and where to look. They told him when to turn and how to do it, how to maintain the correct airspeed and how to lower the landing gear. Sitting at home listening to all this on the radio was nerve-racking enough – one can imagine what it must have been like in the simulator. There was a moment when the 'pilot' began to lose control on the final approach, but he regained it at the last moment and 'landed' the aircraft safely. At least in theory it landed safely, because the pilot on the 'ground' still maintained that the jolt on landing would have fractured all the passengers' spines, even if the aircraft had landed intact. We shall never know – until it actually happens. But it is very unlikely to happen, because there is always a co-pilot equally capable of flying the aircraft and sometimes the flight engineer is also a pilot.

While the flight crew are involved in the business of flying there are two pieces of equipment going silently about their own work. The first is a flight data recorder, a small box, proofed against fire, water and impact shocks and fitted with an underwater beacon to aid recovery. It records speed, height, 'g' and heading against a common time base. Most aircraft carry a device capable of recording many more parameters which is then termed a flight recorder. The second is a Cockpit Voice Recorder (CVR), which continuously records the last 30 minutes of flight deck conversation and radio transmissions. These have proved invaluable on several occasions as the only record of what happened before an accident. They provide vital information when an inquest is held and are often the only way of determining exactly what went wrong. They also give an indication of those rare occasions when a warning system has not alerted the flight crew, who are unaware of a failure in the aircraft systems. There have been occasions when an aircraft has crashed but there has been no indication of the crew being aware of any impending disaster before impact. Just in case they do notice, however, there are life jackets stowed behind the seats and oxygen masks for each member of the crew in case of fire or de-pressurization. Having tried to recover the aircraft, grabbed their life jackets and looked to the safety of the passengers, if the crew are still in one piece, there is an escape hatch for emergency exit from the flight deck.

*Although smaller and more compact, the flight deck of the Anglo-French Concorde is very similar to that of the 747. It is fitted with an almost identical range of instruments, making it easier and more economical to maintain.*

# Weather

A pilot can get some idea of the weather conditions ahead simply by looking out through the windshield of the aircraft. He can judge areas of possible turbulence by cloud formation but he cannot tell for certain what is ahead, particularly at night. To find out exactly what the weather has in store for him he looks at his Weather Radar Screen. On this screen areas of rain and storm are depicted by a phosphorescent map. The pilot can steer a path round these areas or choose a route where turbulence is at a minimum, if he is forced to follow a course through the bad weather.

The radar system is operated by feeding a very powerful source of electrical energy in short bursts along a hollow tube, or 'waveguide', to the nose of the aircraft. The energy is then concentrated into a fine beam by a reflector dish or 'scanner'. The scanner swings from side to side causing the beam to sweep from side to side through the air ahead of the aircraft. Between bursts of energy which send the beam out the system listens for a reply. During these intervals transmitted energy is reflected back by droplets of water in the cloud formations ahead. The scanner picks up this message beam, which is reflected into the waveguide and amplified to produce a visual display on the screen.

It is as hazardous to fly too close to a storm as it is to travel through it. A Southern Airways DC-9 en route for Atlanta crashed while trying to make an emergency landing on a State highway in severe weather conditions. All power was lost in the two rear-mounted engines and the pilot was unable to restart them. Sixty-two passengers were killed and the aircraft destroyed. The National Transportation Safety Board determined that the loss of thrust was due to 'ingestion of massive amounts of water and hail which, in combination with thrust lever movement, induced severe stalling in and major damage to the engine compressors'. The pilot of the DC-9 did not receive any prior warning of the storm and was relying on weather radar.

Looking at the screen, the pilot may be confronted by a variety of cloud formation in his path. To determine which are potentially dangerous he operates a 'contour' switch. When selected the contour mode singles out any clouds above a certain signal strength and removes them from the display. The less hospitable clouds are left with dark interiors. Where an outline is most clearly defined or contoured, this indicates the very worst conditions. These are the cloud areas that the pilot will avoid because it is here that he is most likely to come up against severe turbulence. The latest sets use colour to distinguish varying levels of precipitation.

Another facility on the screen available to the pilot is the 'map' mode of operation. In this capacity the narrow beam used for the weather radar is deflected downwards by the scanner and made to fan out by the use of additional deflectors. Land and water reflect the beam differently, producing a much darker area where water occurs. Extremes of terrain and clearly defined lines such as a coastline show up much better than a flat plain or rolling country with no distinguishing features. Mountains appear as dark patches and the pilot must take care not to confuse these with lakes or sea, which will show in a similar way on the screen. The mountains themselves reflect bright patches on the display but block the passage of the beam, creating a dark patch which shows on the screen.

A pilot would not try to steer the aircraft by the mapping facility but he would find it useful for confirming his position. If his other instruments indicate that he should be over the coast of Florida, he can reassure himself by looking at the screen. If there is a clean line representing the coast and a dark patch of sea, he knows he is in the right part of the world. If there is no sign of either — he may very well be lost.

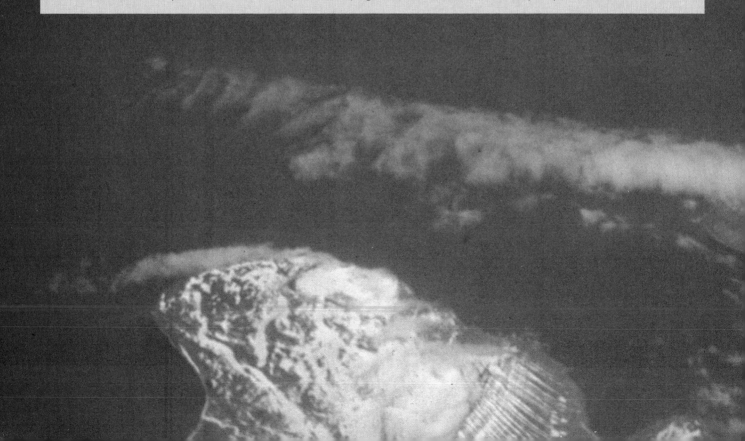

# Safety and Maintenance

Running an international airline with a large fleet of jet aircraft requires a very considerable capital investment — not only in the aircraft themselves, which can cost over $50,000,000 each, but in back-up facilities to keep them in the air. The safety regulations and certification requirements for aircraft are among the strictest of any industry in the world. No new type of aircraft can carry passengers commercially until it has received its Certificate of Airworthiness. Minimum requirements are laid down for testing every aspect of the new aircraft's design and construction. Concorde's delta-wing configuration underwent 5,000 hours in the wind tunnel as part of its acceptance. Instruments, tyres, windshield glass and even upholstery fabric are all subject to scrutiny and must conform to the standards laid down by the various national and international aviation bodies.

The standards themselves have to be revised from time to time as new knowledge and information becomes available about the potential hazards to safety in the air. New types of aircraft require new lines of thought on safety. Wilbur and Orville Wright, flying at 48 km/h (30 mph), had none of the problems of metal fatigue and 'cracks' which have plagued the operators of the 1960s and 1970s. Despite this, however, the industry has learnt a great deal and has so far not failed to cope with the problems it has set itself in the brief 77 years it has taken to double the speed of sound.

As the 1950s saw the first effects of metal fatigue on pressurized turbojet aircraft, so the 1970s have had to contend with new problems of stress, notably in the form of the notorious 'crack'. The actual causes of cracks — particularly in wings, tailplanes and engine pylons — are still being debated. However, there is little doubt that whether caused by incorrect handling of the parts concerned or by stress, fatigue can weaken the structure further if allowed to set in and this can be the cause of malfunction and possible disaster. The only solution at present, apart from preventing the cracks forming in the first place, is to be sure they are detected, as soon as they occur. This requires very sophisticated X-ray and ultra-sonic equipment that can detect a

*Flight instruments are serviced in special dust-free laboratories at the Qantas Jet Base in Sydney.*

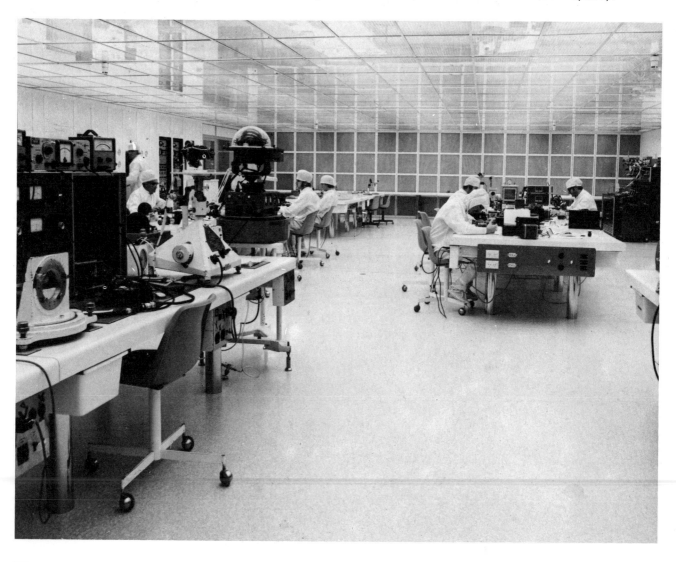

crack in a structure in the same way it can a broken bone. Dyes and magnetic particles are also used in the detection of certain types of cracks, many of which are in fact better described as scratches. The popular idea of gaping fissures in the wing section of an aircraft is a great exaggeration.

Few people would have thought in 1952 that the beautiful new Comet was soon to claim so many lives. By April 1954, three had broken up in flight and designers had to take a close look at the materials they were using and the stresses the aircraft were being asked to withstand. The world's first turbojet airliner proved an invaluable lesson in understanding the problems of fatigue in pressurized jet aircraft. Modifications were made to the fuselage design in an attempt to cure the problem and there are still Comets in service today. In some respects the design is still undated and in its day had an aerodynamic look which was years ahead of its time.

More recently the loss of an American Airlines DC-10 at Chicago O'Hare has provided a similar pointer to the aircraft designer and operators. In one of the most publicized air disasters of all time, the port engine pylon came away from the wing on take-off, depositing the engine on the ground. Damage to the hydraulic system is thought to have caused a wing stall, which in turn caused the aircraft to crash. Two hundred and seventy people were killed as a result. The press immediately stirred up a panic about the aircraft's design, which until then had had a respectable record. The aircraft was grounded temporarily on all routes and each and every operator set about inspecting his aircraft. The results are well known – a number of aircraft were found to have cracks, some larger than others, in the engine pylons. The lesson may have been expensive in terms of human life but it was a lesson quickly learnt. It required a close look at the design of the pylon, a very close look at the methods used for maintaining the aircraft – particularly concerning the replacement of engines – and it has brought into question the procedures adopted in situations where power is lost on take-off. Theorists are now questioning recommended procedures for climb after take-off, in the event of trouble, particularly concerning the target airspeed.

The DC-10 disaster demonstrated very clearly a fundamental problem in determining and averting faults. It was not necessarily negligence that caused the cracked pylon to be overlooked, however it may have been caused in the first place. It was more a question of not knowing what to look for or where. It is easy in retrospect for critics to say that such things should be obvious, but all the knowledge that exists concerning aircraft safety and performance has had to be gained from experience. Theories may be correct but they must still be proven in the field.

Thanks to the Comet, we have a greater understanding of aerodynamics and the problems of metal fatigue. Thanks to the Boeing 707, we know more about tailplane design. And thanks to the DC-10, we now know how cracks can develop and – even more important – where they can occur. The 707 probably now has the safest tailplane design of any aircraft flying, and the DC-10 will probably soon have the safest pylon design in the light of experience.

## Fail-safe

The design of an aircraft is required to satisfy two simple fundamental rules: the first is that no single significant failure of any part or system subject to failure shall cause any distress or hazard either to the aircraft or its occupants; the second is that a second significant failure on the same flight, other than on take-off, shall leave the aircraft comfortably capable of being brought to a safe landing by a pilot of even below-average competence. In many cases there are secondary and even tertiary systems to take over if a fault occurs. Where an engine fails, the aircraft must still be able to fly on its remaining engines – and this ruling applies to every transport aircraft including those with only two engines. Certification includes tests to prove that the aircraft is in fact capable of meeting the rules.

A great deal obviously rests on the resourcefulness and skill of the pilot. Naturally there are exceptions. No one could blame either pilot or aircraft when an ill-starred 707 had its wing ripped off

*A British Airways 747 undergoing maintenance in one of the airline's hangars at London's Heathrow airport.*

by turbulence over Mount Fuji while flying through a cloudless blue sky.

Safety and maintenance are very closely bound together. The manufacturer of every aircraft type lays down exactly how particular maintenance procedures should be carried out. He tells the airline how to dismantle various parts and how often components should be inspected and tested, serviced or replaced. The degree of inspection and the scale of the overhaul varies according to the number of flying hours. Routine checks are done about every 50 flying hours. More extensive checks are done every 500-700 hours and progressively major overhauls are carried out up to every 14,000 hours. The major ones can take several weeks, while every part of the aircraft is checked inside and out.

During major overhauls the fuselage and wing sections are inspected and screened for signs of corrosion, stress and fatigue, the engines are removed and stripped down and instrumentation is taken away to special dust-free laboratories. Here all the instruments are tested for accuracy. A log of the crew's comments and complaints is examined and any reports of problems experienced with any system are looked into. The aircraft is cleaned as well. Dirty aircraft are expensive on fuel consumption. Dirt accumulating on the fuselage can affect the aircraft's performance and increase drag in flight, thus requiring considerably more fuel to maintain airspeed.

## Space and equipment

Just how serious a business it is to maintain a fleet of jet aircraft is demonstrated by the facilities in which the various airlines have invested. British Airways have extensive facilities at London Heathrow where they service and maintain not only their own fleet but other airlines' as well. Most airlines are only too willing to share their facilities under contract with other operators in order to spread the enormous cost of equipment and ground space. Every time a new aircraft type is delivered the appropriate maintenance equipment must also be purchased. A wide-bodied jet with a tail-mounted engine such as the TriStar will require different access platforms and lifting gear to the narrow-bodied 707 with wing-mounted engines The

sheer bulk of the 747 requires much larger accommodation than the much smaller DC-9 or Trident.

When British Airways took delivery of their fleet of L-1011 TriStars they commissioned special extension gantries to be built on to the existing maintenance hangars. These gantries slide apart on wheels to allow the aircraft to be towed into the hangar. They are then slid back into position to fit round the tail section of the aircraft for engine maintenance. British Airways also have five Concordes at present, which require individual facilities. (The airline is expected to take delivery of a further three in due course.) The huge delta wing makes it very difficult to get close to the fuselage without actually stepping on the delicate wing itself. The answer is an ingenious 'jigsaw piece' platform with a cutaway down the centre. The aircraft is towed into the slot so that the platform fits neatly round the fuselage, with padded buffers along each edge to protect the body of the aircraft. The wings fit underneath the platform so that maintenance engineers can walk across and work on the fuselage without fear of damaging the wings.

Another problem with Concorde is putting on a spare tyre. It requires more than a jack and a spanner to replace a wheel. The answer is another ingenious idea. The aircraft is parked with its wheels standing on metal platforms set into the floor of the hanger. Sturdy support jacks are placed under the aircraft. The metal platforms are then lowered into the floor, leaving the aircraft on the jacks and the undercarriage hanging free. The engineers can then climb down into the pits and work on the landing gear and change the tyres with comparative ease.

One of the most impressive aircraft maintenance installations is under construction at the new Singapore airport of Changi. Singapore Airlines, the national flag-carriers, have spent S$178,000,000 on their new maintenance facility. It is the world's largest pillar-free hangar, with a ground space equivalent to seven football pitches. It has extensive part and spares storage in addition to the usual maintenance equipment, excellent fire-fighting equipment and first-class staff facilities. Singapore Airways operate a large international fleet including 747s and one Concorde, which flies London–Bahrain–Singapore in conjunction with British Airways.

No airline can afford a base like Changi at every major destination point, if at all. It is far more practical for airlines with similar aircraft in their fleet to get together and do a deal. Quick turn-arounds do not require any major overhauls, but more complicated repairs and maintenance are much more economically done on the spot under contract by someone else than by flying all the way back from New York to Sydney or Hong Kong for a new set of plugs.

*Maintenance engineers working through a service hatch on the wing section of a Concorde.*

# Mayday!

However safe an aircraft is, there must always be provision for an emergency. The majority of large international airports average at least one alert every day, although a large number are either false alarms or turn out to be very minor incidents. On board the aircraft, each passenger has a life jacket stowed away under the seat. Oxygen masks are located above each seat and these are automatically released if pressurization in the cabin drops below the safety level. In addition to the exits used for normal debarkation there are several emergency exits which can be opened from both inside and out. On some aircraft, such as the L-1011 TriStar, the emergency doors are positioned clear of the wings to allow easy exit. On an aircraft like Concorde this is more difficult to arrange because of the 'chord' of the delta wing. (This is the distance between the two points at the extremities of the arcs of the delta wings.) The emergency exits have to be positioned above the wing area at intervals along the fuselage. Special slides inflate automatically when the doors are opened. Long flat sections lie across the

wing with vertical slides from the edge of the wing to the ground. The slides themselves are immediately convertible into rafts. RFD Inflatables Limited, which manufactures the evacuation equipment for Concorde, carried out a trial evacuation at Filton, in England. With only 3 'crew' in attendance, 128 'passengers' were evacuated in only 86 seconds – 4 seconds less than the airworthiness regulations' requirement.

## Strictly safe

Whatever the aircraft type, the regulations still apply and these regulations are strict. An inflatable slide must inflate automatically within ten seconds. On a smaller jet such as a BAC One-Eleven it will take three to five seconds, while a larger Concorde equivalent might take eight seconds to inflate. But both are well within the required ten seconds. Emergency evacuation equipment is stowed in the doors so that it can be

automatically activated as soon as the door is opened. The slides are inflated instantly by pressurized gas augmented by air from a built-in injector system.

Life rafts are also standard emergency equipment on all civil aircraft flying long distance. They can be folded up quite small and stowed in a light holdall for portability. They vary slightly in design and size according to the number of people they would be required to hold. The floating section is made of at least two buoyancy chambers, depending on the size of the raft. These are inflated from one cylinder, and some types have special boarding ramps and inflatable seat rings to accommodate up to 36 survivors. The raft is covered with a bright orange canopy to protect the survivors from the elements and the whole thing is constructed of proofed nylon textile.

Every passenger has a life jacket specially designed to cushion the back of the head and keep the face clear of the

*Special evacuation equipment for Concorde by RFD Inflatables Ltd.*

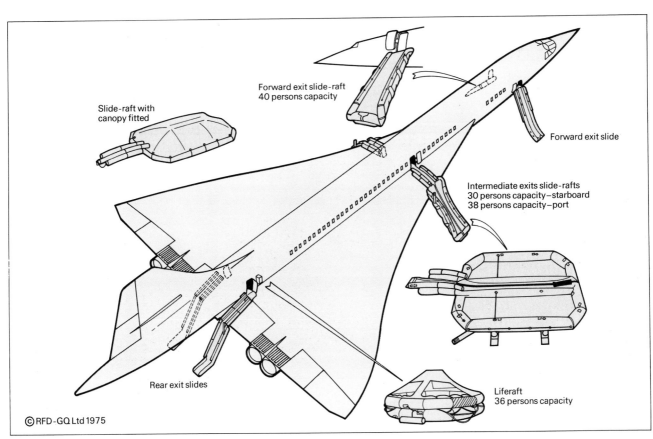

Slide-raft with canopy fitted

Forward exit slide-raft 40 persons capacity

Forward exit slide

Intermediate exits slide-rafts 30 persons capacity – starboard 38 persons capacity – port

Rear exit slides

Liferaft 36 persons capacity

© RFD-GQ Ltd 1975

water. Life jackets are made of synthetic materials in bright orange or yellow for easy recognition in the water. Initially a cylinder inflates the jacket, which can then be topped up by blowing into a tube with a valve. Some jackets are fitted with attention-seeking equipment such as a whistle and a battery-powered light which will last about 20 hours. Smaller models are made for young children with a lifeline to attach to an adult.

Special emergency packs are also carried aboard every aircraft. The contents of these packs vary according to the climate in which the aircraft is expected to be flying. Standard equipment includes distress signals and blue marker dye to put in the water around the raft, a first-aid kit, a compass, water-purifying tablets, fishing equipment, sea-sickness pills, fire-making tablets, a can-opener and various knives with a sharpening stone. Packs for tropical climates also include insect and shark repellants. There is also a baler to empty water from the raft and a survival pamphlet detailing how to survive in various climates.

*An old aircraft being used for an emergency drill with a heavy duty foam tender in action.*

## Rough ride

The crew members are all thoroughly trained in how to deal with an emergency and how to use the evacuation and survival equipment. Before they start flying they take part in practice evacuations and learn how to use the life rafts, usually in a swimming pool. They must know exactly where to find fire extinguishers, oxygen and carbon dioxide cylinders, fireproof gloves, axes, goggles, torches and ropes, all of which are stowed on board the aircraft in case they are needed.

There are many things which can cause an emergency — some more noticeable to the passenger than others. In many cases, only the pilot and crew are aware of anything out of the ordinary occurring. In a few cases, even the pilot himself is not aware until it is too late. Burst tyres on landing might give the passengers a nasty jolt but they probably would not be aware of what had actually happened. A 747 landing at London Heathrow one afternoon blew one tyre which in turn caused the other three closest to it to blow. Despite the loud bang heard by onlookers, the aircraft gave no indication of losing control or even shuddering. The passengers

probably put it down to a bumpy landing and thought no more of it.

Passengers are far more likely to notice turbulence during flight. This can range from a few bumps to an aircraft turning through a 180° roll and finishing upside down, in the more extreme cases. This actually occurred once but miraculously, the pilot managed to recover control of the aircraft and land safely. There have been occasions when aircraft have suddenly dropped like a stone by several hundred, or even thousand, feet in a patch of severe turbulence. The effect on the passengers is like having the aircraft whipped out from underneath them. Any loose objects such as glasses, hand luggage and meal trays are sent flying around the cabin and passengers have been known to sustain severe injuries because they have not been strapped into their seats.

Under very extreme conditions engines and wings have been ripped clean off the fuselage but obviously this is an extremely remote occurrence. Weather conditions on this scale can usually be detected by radar and the aircraft either re-routes to avoid the problem area or simply does not fly. However, there are certain types of turbulence which even escape the roving eye of the radar. Clear air turbulence (CAT) is one example. This is undetect-

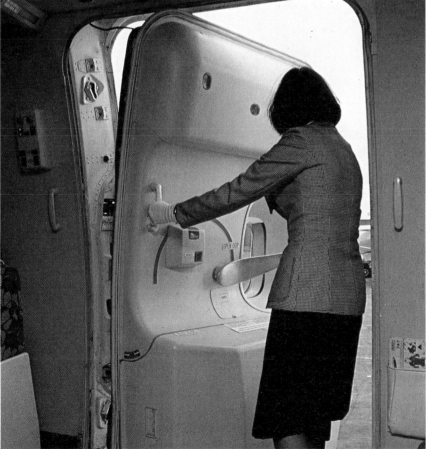

able on the weather radar screen and is far worse for the unsuspecting passenger than it is for the pilot. The effect of CAT is that of an aircraft being dragged across a rocky terrain on its belly at high speed. The condition is caused by two conflicting currents of air meeting at speed at high altitude. The effect can be quite unnerving but, in fact, it is by no means as dangerous as it might appear and the pilot can simply take evasive action by seeking a lower altitude to get clear of it. He will never try to climb above a patch of turbulence as it may well extend far above the maximum altitude capability of the aircraft. Concorde is one aircraft which has an excellent reputation for smooth flying. Because of its high altitude cruise capability of 50,000–60,000 ft, Concorde rides above the majority of turbulence and passengers only experience a fraction of the discomfort felt in a subsonic aircraft.

Mountain ranges can be dangerous areas when turbulence is present. On the downward side an aircraft can be sucked down, even with the engines at full power in an attempt to pull out of it. A pilot is faced with a formidable task in remaining completely calm and in control. If he were to panic during his attempt to recover the aircraft the chances are that he would fail. The comforting fact remains that pilots are minutely screened and examined before they are licensed to fly. The qualities most sought after in a pilot, apart from the obvious ability to fly an aircraft, are ones of calm and control. A sudden upset can send all the instruments on the flight deck berserk and, although this occurs only infrequently, on the one occasion when it does the pilot must not be tempted into sudden corrective measures at high speed to bring the aircraft under control. Engine speed is eased back and rudder, elevator and ailerons are used with discretion to hold the aircraft as level as possible until the storm has been weathered. A sudden, uncoordinated action on the part of a desperate pilot would be more likely to spell disaster than the storm itself.

Turbulence can also affect the handling of an aircraft, causing it to 'stall', resulting in a sudden, drastic loss of lift. This is caused by a disturbance in the smooth flow of air which supports the aircraft, creating small whirlpools and ripples. Every modern aircraft has a built-in warning against stalling, in the form of a 'stick-shaker'. If a stall is near the control stick starts to shake under

*Above left Foam being sprayed from a hand-held nozzle.*
*Left Cabin crew opening one of the emergency exits aboard an aircraft.*

the pilot's hand. The remedy is to push the stick forward, causing the aircraft to dive, and to increase the speed until it has recovered from the near-stall condition. Aircraft are affected differently according to their design. One with a high-set tail and rear engine installation will behave differently from one with wing-mounted engines and a low tailplane. The stall qualities of the first generation jet transports were good. They degraded with the second generation when maximum lift appeared to override good handling qualities, but they returned to good again with the latest wide-bodies and Jumbos.

In addition to the stick-shaker, some aircraft are fitted with an additional safety device called a 'stick-pusher'. This is activated automatically by signals which are initiated by the disrupted airflow around the wing of the aircraft. In simple terms, the device detects when all is not well and informs the stick-shaker to warn the pilot as described. Following this, the stick-pusher actually takes control of the aircraft, forcing the stick forward into a corrective dive. The incidence of complete stall is rare — about one in every 100,000 flights, and even then the aircraft is usually recovered without damage.

An aircraft design undergoes thousands of hours of testing for stress before it can be considered ready to be applied to a production model. But no aircraft, particularly one weighing 82–102 tonnes (80–100 tons), was designed to be bent double. A 707 flying through clear weather near Mount Fuji was suddenly caught in a patch of undetected turbulence caused by the 'rotor' effect down-wind of the peak. The strain on the aircraft was more than it was designed to withstand and it broke up in mid-air, losing first a wing, then the front section of the fuselage. Needless to say, there were no survivors. However, occurrences on this scale are few

and although stories such as the Mount Fuji disaster may be enough to put many people off flying for life, the statistics are still undeniably encouraging.

It is estimated that flying is 25 times safer than crossing a busy road. Airworthiness authorities are in general agreement that, in 1979, the western-world public transport fatal accident rate was two per million flights. Like all statistics, this rate has to be handled intelligently. If fate decrees you are to die in an aircraft accident, it could well be on your very first flight. But if we work on averages as the only way of excluding the randomness of life, then the above rate means that you would have to make half a million flights before being involved in a fatal accident.

No aircraft is given its certificate of airworthiness until it has undergone exhaustive tests, and the requirements for minimum handling abilities are heavy. The irony of flying is that a passenger will breathe a sigh of relief as the aircraft taxies to a halt, climb into his car and take off again on the most dangerous part of his journey — driving home.

Right *While an engineer examines a damaged tyre, the aircraft is supported by inflatable concertina lifting equipment which is positioned under the wing sections of the aircraft. One such device can be seen in the background behind the engineer. As it inflates it lifts the entire aircraft until it is clear of the ground for recovery.*

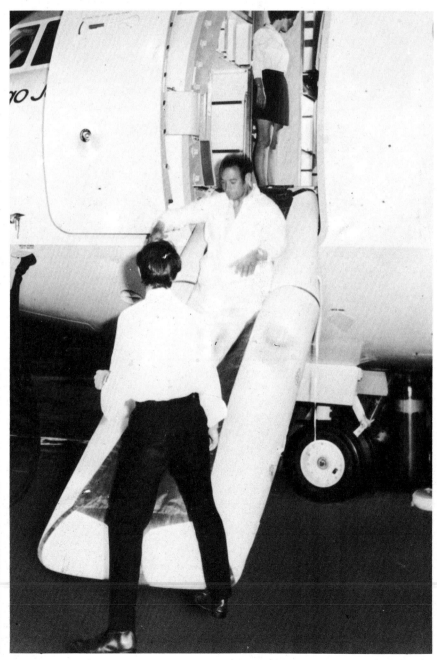

Right *Evacuation slide for the BAC One-Eleven by RFD Inflatables Ltd.* Below *Concorde slide-raft (for 40) holding 53; also by RFD Inflatables.*

The short to medium range Boeing 727 is the world's best-selling civil airliner.

# Aircraft and Airlines

# The Jet Engine

When one considers how much an average civil aircraft weighs it is a very remarkable feat of engineering to propel it 10 km (6 miles) high at a speed of 950 km/h (600 mph). It is even more remarkable to consider Concorde, which can travel at more than double that speed and which proves what a truly remarkable development the jet engine is. The first design was conceived by Frank Whittle in the 1930s and its early applications were on military aircraft, which have often been the proving ground for later, civil applications. The supersonic Olympus 593 engine developed by Rolls Royce and SNECMA for Concorde began its life as a subsonic power unit for the Vulcan bomber.

## More sociable engines

Gradually, and in particular during the last ten years, concern for the environment has become more and more prominent a consideration in the design of aircraft engines. Fuel costs have risen dramatically and it is no longer feasible to operate with engines which drink vast quantities of expensive jet fuel. The latest generation of subsonic jets are both quieter and more economical than ever before and far more efficient than their propellered predecessors.

The basic principle of the jet engine is simple. Air is taken in through the front and forced out through the back at high velocity. This creates 'thrust', which literally pushes the aircraft forward in the same way that a child's balloon will dart rapidly away when the air is released from the mouthpiece. Thrust is measured in kilos (lbs), and therefore the more powerful the engine the greater the thrust and the faster it can propel the aircraft. The weight of the aircraft is also an important factor. Obviously far greater thrust will be required to lift a 747 carrying 400 passengers off the ground

*The Rolls-Royce RB211 engine, one of a new generation of quieter, more economical turbofans.*

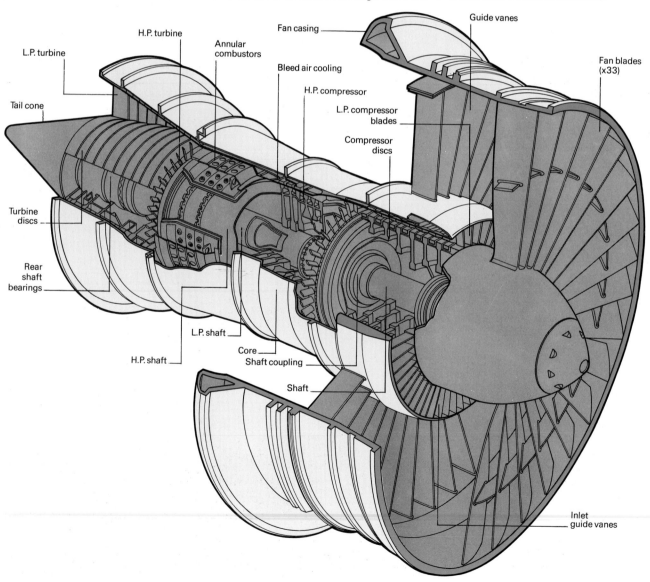

L.P. turbine

H.P. turbine

Annular combustors

Fan casing

Guide vanes

Bleed air cooling

Fan blades (x33)

Tail cone

H.P. compressor

L.P. compressor blades

Compressor discs

Turbine discs

Rear shaft bearings

L.P. shaft

Core

Shaft coupling

Shaft

H.P. shaft

Inlet guide vanes

than would be necessary to get a small business jet with only four passengers airborne.

The jet engine is a highly efficient power-plant compared with the piston engine. There are comparatively few moving parts in a turbine engine and, unlike a propeller, it remains efficient at high subsonic speeds. Additionally, jet engines start their lives quite conservatively rated and then develop potential in terms of thrust in the range of +10% to +50%. As examples, a Rolls-Royce RB211-524B at 22,700 kg (50,000 lb) of thrust will quite soon grow to 25,000 kg (55,000 lb), and the long-established Pratt & Whitney JT8D has increased its thrust by about 50% in its long life. Apart from Rolls-Royce and Pratt & Whitney, there is a third major jet engine manufacturer, General Electric. Rolls are based in the United Kingdom while the latter two both operate from the United States. Between the three of them these companies are responsible for the supply of the majority of civil aircraft engines.

A jet engine looks so smooth and uncomplicated from the outside that it is hard to conceive how it can produce so much power. The main components of the 'pure' jet are the compressor, the combustion chambers, the turbine and the jet nozzle. Air enters the engine through the inlet duct which sometimes contains inlet guide vanes. The compressor itself lies behind these vanes and the air is compressed as it passes

Below right *A Rolls-Royce/SNECMA Olympus engine removed from a Concorde for maintenance.*
Below *The effect of reversed thrust on the flow of air through an engine.*

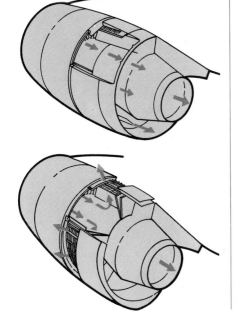

through. The pressurized air is then forced into the combustion chambers which are set in a circle beyond the compressor. Here the air is mixed with fuel and ignited, which causes massive heat and considerable increase in the volume of the resultant gases. This causes the gases to leave the combustion chambers at high speed and to pass through a turbine which turns as a result. Not all the air is used in burning the fuel, which is injected continuously into the chambers. About three-quarters of the air acts as a coolant to control the temperature of the gas and that of the combustion chambers themselves.

By activating the turbine the gases are in fact powering the compressor where the cycle first began, because it is the motion of the turbine which powers the compressor. The gases carry on through the jet nozzle, which is 'convergent' in shape. This means the gases are forced out through a small outlet which creates high-exhaust velocity. The effect of this, as the gases pass out into the atmosphere, is to create the thrust which propels the engine, and therefore the aircraft, forward.

There are variations on this basic principle. Some engines have two compressors, or 'spools', instead of one – a low-pressure one and a high-pressure one. This type is known as a twin-spool, of which the Concorde Olympus power unit is an example. Pure jet engines are thirsty by comparison with the far more economical 'by-pass' engines and this design is becoming almost universally adopted by manufacturers. Only a small proportion of air entering a by-pass engine actually passes through the combustion chamber and turbine. The majority of it is 'by-passed' round through a special annular duct surrounding the engine and is propelled by a large multi-bladed fan housed at the front of the engine. This, like the compressor, is driven by a turbine and serves the dual role of assisting air-intake to the compressor and acting as a propellor as on an 'old-fashioned' aircraft. The actual design of by-pass engines varies.

## Reverse thrust

It is an achievement in itself to get an aircraft airborne at speeds of up to 2,170 km/h (1,350 mph). Having done that, it takes a great deal to stop it again when the aircraft lands. While the brakes on the wheels contribute most to the slowing-down action, a significant contribution is also made by 'thrust reversal'. Thrust, pushed out the back of the engine to propel it forwards, is obstructed and made to turn round and push the other way, effectively pushing the aircraft backwards. This acts against the airspeed of the aircraft and produces a braking effect. Reverse thrust is achieved by revolving shell-shaped 'buckets' which move into the path of the exhaust gases which hit the screen and are deflected back along the outside of the engine in a forward direction.

There is seldom any need to look at an aircraft engine as it lands to know that it is in reverse thrust. The noise will give it away immediately. There are ways of reducing the noise, to a certain extent, by modifying the shape of the exhaust, but this results in loss of power. The fan-jet is quieter and more economical than the pure jet and is not, therefore, fitted with any form of silencer.

Precisely where the engines are mounted on the aircraft depends on the aircraft's design. On some aircraft all the engines are wing-mounted. This means the engines are attached to the underside of the aircraft's wing by means of a 'pylon', as on the 707, DC-8, 747, Airbus, 737, 757 and 767. Rear-mounted engines are grouped around the tail section of the aircraft, either one on each side as on the Caravelle, BAC One-Eleven and the DC-9, or one on each side with a third set into the tail as on the Trident and the 727. A third combination allows for one engine at the rear, set into the tail, plus one on each wing as on the L-1011 TriStar and the DC-10. There are two aircraft which carry twin engines on each side of the tail – the British VC-10 and the Russian IL-62.

# Through the Sound Barrier

Concorde – in many people's eyes the greatest achievement ever in civil air transport – has become the most prestigious executive jet ever. Built jointly by British Aerospace and Aérospatiale, it has finally proved that the ordinary man can travel safely at twice the speed of sound without any ill effects.
Inset left *Concorde passengers check in at special desks where they are dealt with quickly.*
Inset right *First class comfort aboard a British Airways Concorde. Despite the narrow fuselage, every passenger has ample room.*

The first truly supersonic aircraft to see service in the West was built in the United States. The F-100 Super Sabre first flew in 1953 and was followed by a succession of other supersonic aircraft, but these were all designed for military service. It was 20 years before the public viewed the West's first supersonic civil aircraft. In September 1973, Concorde 02 touched down at Orly, near Paris, after completing the fastest trans-Atlantic crossing ever made by a commercial aircraft. It took exactly 3 hours 33 minutes to fly from Dulles, Washington, to Orly, at an average speed of 1,800 km/h (1,100 mph) which is equivalent to 30 km (18 miles) per minute.

The original project to build a supersonic transport aircraft was begun in Britain in 1943 but this was cancelled after only a few years' research. There was considerable anxiety about the effects of supersonic travel on both the aircraft and the passengers aboard. In 1956 research was resumed under the auspices of the Supersonic Transport Aircraft Committee (STAC). Meanwhile, France had also begun studying the feasibility of a supersonic transport aircraft on similar lines to the British. After extensive negotiations an agreement was signed between the two countries

in November 1962 to undertake a joint development programme that was to lead to the building of Concorde.

The United States and the Soviet Union were not idle during this period. The American supersonic transport aircraft programme (SST) was taken as far as the design stage and orders were already being discussed when political pressure intervened to call a halt to it. The Russian TU-144 fared better in that it reached production stage although a demonstration aircraft crashed at the Paris Air Show in 1973. Gradually the aircraft was withdrawn, first from passenger, then from cargo service. No news was heard of any consequence until November 1979 when mention was made of the TU-144D. This improved version has a proposed range of 7,000 km (4,350 miles) with a 50% reduction in fuel consumption. No further details were available at the time of writing, however, there is talk of resurrecting the American project.

Supersonic flight presented the designers with new problems not encountered with subsonic aircraft. The first problem was to design an airframe capable of withstanding the stress and high temperatures created at speeds in excess of 1,600 km/h (1,000 mph). Another problem was to find a power

unit efficient enough to meet the demands of flying both subsonically and supersonically. The airframe had to handle satisfactorily at minimum speeds, including landing and take-off, yet incur minimum drag at supersonic speeds. To achieve this the now-familiar streamlined fuselage and beautiful delta wing configuration was evolved. Long before the prototype flew, the basic configuration underwent exhaustive ground testing involving more than 5,000 hours in the wind tunnel. Various modifications at different stages perfected the final design.

## Interim solution

One improvement was the addition of the droopable nose and visor, which can be lowered to allow maximum pilot visibility on landing and take-off and raised during supersonic flight to maintain the streamlined shape of the fuselage and protect the flight deck windscreen. This arrangement was a highly original concept, but only designed as an interim solution to be solved by other means at a later stage. It proved so successful, however, that it was adopted as a permanent feature. The design of the tail section also underwent modification. Extending and re-shaping it resulted in significant reductions in drag at supersonic speed and also increased the overall fuel capacity.

Another major decision to be taken was the choice of material from which to construct the airframe. Aluminium alloy was finally chosen as the basic structural material. Thousands of samples of this alloy underwent extensive tests for fatigue strength and resistance to corrosion. Metal has a tendency to 'creep' when subjected to extremes of temperature and mechanical loading. This means that the metal becomes deformed and its shape distorted – a problem always present in any aircraft design. All the materials used in Concorde underwent similar tests, including titanium, stainless steel, paints, plastics and special glazing for the cabin windows, which are smaller than on a conventional subsonic aircraft.

## The Olympus engine

Concorde is powered by four Olympus 593 twin-spool turbojets. The engine was designed in Bristol, England, after the Second World War, to power what

*The droopable nose solved the problem of visibility at low speed and protection at supersonic cruise.*

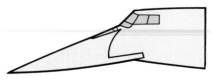

Nose and visor up

Nose up and visor down

Nose at intermediate droop

Nose at full droop

*By the use of fuel transfer the centre of gravity of the aircraft can be adjusted to suit different speeds.*

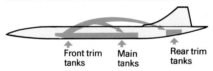

Rearward transfer for transonic acceleration

Front trim tanks    Main trim tanks    Rear trim tanks

Emergency deceleration transfer

Forward transfer for end of cruise

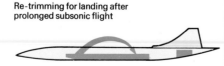

Re-trimming for landing after prolonged subsonic flight

became the Vulcan bomber. It was further developed to supersonic capability and a special 'annular' combustion chamber was fitted to reduce the excessive smoke that was expelled on landing and take-off. Once again, new materials had to be found for the construction of the supersonic engine. Like the airframe, it would be subjected to far greater extremes of temperature than its subsonic equivalent. Titanium and nickel-based alloys were chosen to cope with this problem, the latter being used to resist the highest temperatures in the combustion chamber, turbine blades and reheat assembly.

The engine has various special features that were developed specifically for use on Concorde. These include a specially designed intake and exhaust system. In very simple terms, air enters the engine through the intake system, which features a 'variable geometry'. This means that moveable ramps in the roof of the intake and a 'spill door', incorporating intake flaps, in the floor automatically adjust to maximum area to provide maximum air flow to the engine during take-off. At speeds above Mach 1.3 (1,390 km/h/860 mph) the ramps start to lower automatically to control the position of the shock wave and reduce the air velocity at the engine face. If an engine has to be shut down in supersonic flight, air is spilled overboard through the spill door in the floor of the intake and the ramps are lowered to their maximum position.

The exhaust system also features variable geometry, a reheat system normally installed only on military aircraft, and a thrust reversing system common to most civil aircraft. The main engine hot gas flow terminates in a variable

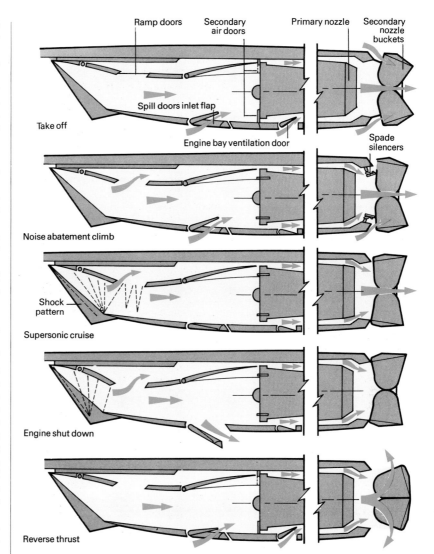

Above *Airflow through the variable geometry intake and exhaust systems of the Olympus engine.*

Below *Distribution of fuel tanks aboard Concorde. (cf. fuel transfer system illustrated on page 104).*

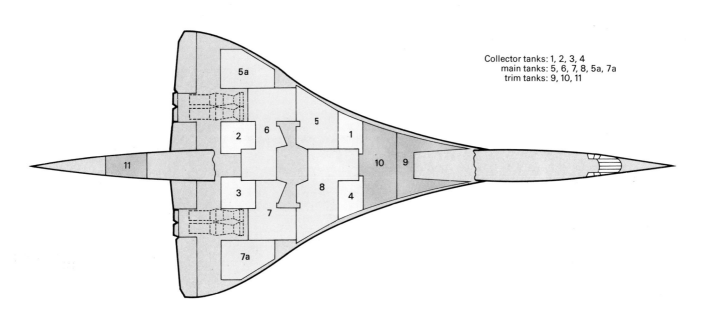

Collector tanks: 1, 2, 3, 4
main tanks: 5, 6, 7, 8, 5a, 7a
trim tanks: 9, 10, 11

area primary nozzle which is necessary to permit simultaneous achievement of required engine speed and gas temperatures over a wide range of intake temperatures. To provide extra thrust for take-off and transonic acceleration a reheat system is fitted which works in conjunction with the primary nozzle. This simply burns fuel in the exhaust and is an efficient way of achieving extra thrust without scaling up either the size of the engine or its operating parameters. At the aft end of the exhaust system is a combined variable area secondary nozzle and thrust reverser system. A variable secondary nozzle is required for efficient expansion of the main engine hot gas flow to provide the widely differing pressure ratios between, for example, take-off conditions and supersonic cruise. The thrust reversers are two clamshell buckets which, in forward thrust, are open and allow the gases to exhaust between them. In reverse thrust, used to slow the aircraft during the landing run, the buckets close and deflect the gas stream forwards at angles which allow it to pass out through holes in the uppper and lower nozzle surfaces.

## Mach 2

Concorde has been designed to cruise at Mach 2 (2,124 km/h (1,320 mph)). This final figure was the result of much debate and deliberation by the designers. The Olympus engines are capable of even higher speeds, but above Mach 2 problems of temperature and overall efficiency make it impractical. The extremes of intake temperature can range from −55°C (−67°F) at subsonic speeds in particularly cold climates to as high as +127°C (293°F) in supersonic flight. Originally Concorde was intended to cruise at Mach 2.2 (2,330 km/h (1,450 mph)) but tests on the aluminium alloys showed this to be the maximum for acceptable short-period temperature limits. The lower speed of Mach 2 was therefore finally agreed upon for a sustained cruise speed.

## Supersonic control

To fly efficiently at supersonic speeds with maximum handling capability the weight distribution within the aircraft must be as finely balanced as the external design. Concorde features an in-flight fuel transfer system to maintain trim. This means the fuel itself is used to maintain trim, within the aircraft, in place of external aerodynamic means which would increase drag at high speeds. In addition to the main tanks, there are front and rear trim tanks from which fuel is pumped backwards or forwards as required. As the aircraft accelerates, fuel is transferred from the front tanks to the main and rear tanks. After supersonic cruise, fuel is transferred back to the front tanks to adjust the centre of gravity for subsonic flight.

## Businessman's jet

Concorde is 62.2 m (204 ft) long with a wing span of 25.6 m (84 ft), 8.2 m (27 ft) shorter than a Boeing 747. It can carry up to 108 passengers and baggage more than 6,300 km (3,900 miles) at a cruising speed of Mach 2 (2,124 km/h (1,320 mph)). Its extremely high cruise altitude of 50,000–60,000 ft and low-drag aerodynamic shape considerably reduce the exposure of passengers to turbulence in flight. A journey from London to New York taking a minimum of 7 hours 5 minutes by subsonic aircraft can be completed in 3 hours 45 minutes supersonically, saving nearly $3\frac{1}{2}$ hours or 47% of flying time. This has proved very popular with business men, whose time is always at a premium. Current operators of Concorde include British Airways and Air France, with Singapore Airlines and Braniff operating services in conjunction with British Airways. Flight schedules are carefully chosen to fit in with business working hours. A morning flight can allow a passenger to attend a lunchtime meeting on the other side of the Atlantic and still be back at his desk the following day. Service aboard is of the highest standard with all passengers flying first class. A survey of passengers revealed that 95% of them thought Concorde either matched up to or exceeded their expectations. So it would seem that flying can be safe and comfortable – even at the speed of a rifle bullet.

*As the West's first supersonic airliner, Concorde made many promotion flights. Here one of the Air France aircraft sits in the spotlights at Hong Kong's Kai Tak Airport during a three-day sales visit in November 1976. The reception was attended by many visitors, including aviation experts from the People's Republic of China.*

# Sitting Comfortably

The days – or perhaps one should say nights – when passengers could settle down in their own beds on a long distance flight. The economics of air travel rarely allow for such luxuries, although a few airlines including JAL and Singapore have recently installed berths on the upper decks of 747s. The Boeing Stratocruiser and the Douglas DC-7 were two aircraft which featured reclining seats and bunk beds for long distance flights. But in the 1950s it could take 16 hours to fly the Atlantic and even then there was a stop to re-fuel on the way.

Today flights are faster and the costs high. The main objective has become to pack as many fare-paying passengers as possible into an aircraft which can be 'turned round' as quickly as possible. When an aircraft is on the ground it is costing money – not just in lost revenue, but in parking fees as well. Airports are like car parks; they charge to land and they charge to park. With the new generation of wide-bodied jets, it is now possible to carry up to 500 passengers on one journey in considerable comfort and word is already abroad of an even larger, 600-seater for the late 1980s.

Fuel economies have improved as the turbojet engine has developed and now the emphasis is on reducing fares. In fact, competition among the airlines for lower fares has developed into full-scale war during the last few years. The standard-bearer for low fares has been Sir Freddie Laker and his Skytrain. He has proved that by cutting out a mountain of unnecessary paperwork and booking procedures fares can be halved. This has enouraged healthy competition between the airlines which, in turn, has allowed more people than ever to take to the air – not just on package holidays to Spain but right across the Atlantic and even, more recently, to the Far East.

## Service and comfort

However competitive the fares may be, an airline still has to offer comfort and good service to attract the passengers. This is particularly true of the business clientele. Many businessmen spend a great deal of their working life globetrotting in aircraft and the word soon gets around as to who has the most to offer and for how much. Passengers who fly regularly become connoisseurs of in-flight service and aircraft performance. Smooth, quiet jets with comfortable seating and pleasant crew are far more likely to hold on to their customers, and the airlines are well aware of this.

The passenger will soon notice if the food is cold or the ashtrays dirty, but he is probably not aware of the amount of time, money and research that goes into getting him from A to B in comfort. When an airline orders a new type of aircraft, great thought goes into details which probably would not even be remarked upon by the passengers. Ask a passenger what colour the seats were and he will probably not remember. Yet even seat coverings are carefully chosen to blend in with a final harmonious effect on entering the aircraft. For some reason, bright yellows and oranges seem to be very popular colours with many airlines, often in rather vivid combination. Top-quality fabrics are always used because over a period of time hundreds of people will be using the seats and they will need to withstand considerable wear. The upholstery is also flame-resistant to reduce the hazard of fire on board an aircraft. Very bad turbulence has a strange habit of tearing lighted cigarettes out of people's hands.

Weight is always an important factor on board an aircraft. Even the weight of the paint on the fuselage can increase the fuel consumption accountably. Therefore, with 500 seats on board and 500 passengers sitting in them, even a few grams per seat can make quite a difference. The latest seating is made on a light alloy and steel frame with polyester foam cushions. Seat covers are removable for cleaning and replacement when they become worn. The seats vary in design, but usually they have pivoted centre arm rests with ashtrays inset and provision for plug-in meal trays. Beside each seat, usually set into the armrest, is a small panel of controls for the passenger to use. There is a buzzer to call the cabin crew, a socket for a headset, a reading-light switch and a selector and volume control for music or film soundtrack. The film is projected on to a screen at the front of the cabin for passengers who choose to watch it. The seats can be reclined for passengers who want to sleep and there is a padded headrest for extra comfort. A triple seat installation can weigh as little as 27 kg (60 lb) but that still means an aircraft-load will weigh between 3,650 kg (8,000 lb) and 4,550 kg (10,000 lb).

## Class distinctions

When an airline decides on the layout of the interior of a new aircraft, two basic decisions must be made first. How many passengers is the aircraft to carry and how many 'classes' will there be? Some economy flights are one-class, particularly on short-haul and shuttle

*Seating arrangements vary according to the operating airline; below are cross-sections of the L-1011 TriStar.*

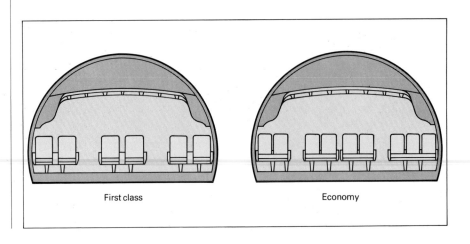

First class            Economy

services. Many passengers will put up with being a little cramped for space if the flight is only one to two hours in duration. The longer the flight, however, the more likely passengers are to want a first-class facility. Business passengers will often fly first-class so that they can arrive fresh and relaxed, possibly carrying on their day's work on board the aircraft. A whole family travelling together to see relatives in Australia would be more likely to want an economy fare. They probably would not be able to afford it otherwise. British Airways have their own 'executive jet' in Concorde. All passengers travel first-class with special check-in facilities and haute cuisine on board.

On narrow-bodied jets such as the Boeing 727 and the Trident, economy seats are three abreast with an aisle down the centre. Smokers are separated from non-smokers at one end of the cabin or seated along one side. In the first-class section the seats are ranged two abreast and are often larger and more lavishly upholstered. Seats are spaced, or 'pitched', 73–81 cm (29–32 in) apart in the economy class cabin, depending on how many passengers are to be fitted in. A more generous allowance of 86–90 cm (34–36 in) is made in the first-class section, but this again depends on how many passengers the airline wants to carry. On a wide-bodied jet the cabin begins to look more like a theatre. The 747 can accommodate two rows of three seats abreast and a third row of four seats abreast, separated by two aisles. The first-class cabin has provision for two double rows of seats and a lounge area on the upper deck where passengers

can relax with a drink – usually free.

Passengers booking in advance can often select which seat they are going to sit in. There are advantages in this – particularly on a daytime flight over the Himalayas or the Grand Canyon. Window seats are invariably the first choice, except possibly by passengers suffering from acrophobia. One passenger who had not flown for many years was determined to sit by a window overlooking the wing so that he could be sure the propellers were still turning. However, aircraft had advanced since he last flew and he found himself booked on a rear-engine turbojet.

## Back to front

Like everything connected with aircraft and flying, there are safety standards set for the design of the seats. Passengers would be a great deal safer if they all faced backwards when flying, but most people prefer to face the way they are going, even when they cannot actually see out. On this particular point the airlines tend to comply with the passengers rather than the experts and as a result there are very few aircraft fitted

today with backward-facing seats. Some older aircraft had seats arranged facing each other in twos with a central table which could be folded down during the flight.

First-class accommodation is usually at the front of the aircraft away from the noise of the engines and the jolt of the landing gear. Aircraft could probably be made even quieter inside than they are at present but a certain amount of noise is desirable, if only to reassure nervous passengers that all the engines are functioning properly. The noisiest part of the aircraft depends on where the engines are mounted. In an aircraft with wing-mounted engines the cabin becomes noisier when sitting level with, or behind, the wings. In an aircraft with tail-mounted engines the noise level does not increase until you reach the rear of the cabin.

This factor and the various 'types' of passenger booked on a flight can be quite a weapon in the hands of vindictive check-in and booking clerks. It has been known for particularly rude, obnoxious passengers to be 'marked' at check-in. The penalty for unsociable behaviour may be an unfortunate mix-up in the seating arrangements with the victim left strategically placed between the toilet and twenty small children on a school holiday.

*All the facilities to service 300 or more passengers must be fitted in as compactly as possible. In addition to the seats, galleys, toilets and baggage racks, there are other pieces of equipment, unseen but vital, which must be fitted in the*

*body of the aircraft. These include the environmental control system which maintains the correct level of oxygen and pressurization within the cabin areas, also cargo holds, fuel tanks, electronics, a power unit and wheel bays.*

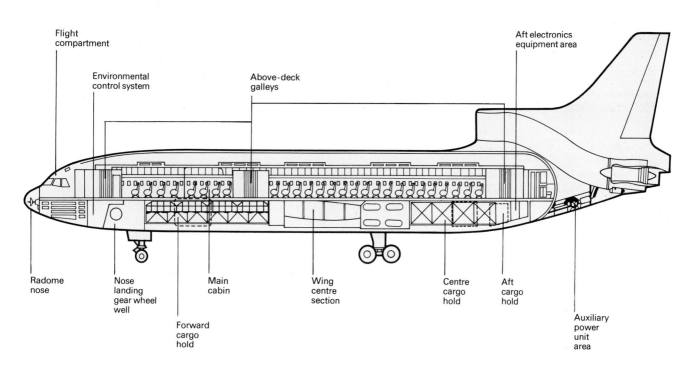

Flight compartment

Environmental control system

Above-deck galleys

Aft electronics equipment area

Radome nose

Nose landing gear wheel well

Forward cargo hold

Main cabin

Wing centre section

Centre cargo hold

Aft cargo hold

Auxiliary power unit area

# Feeding the 5,000

Qantas, the Australian flag carrier, estimate that they serve a full three-course meal plus drinks and snacks to some 5,000 passengers every day. A wide-bodied aircraft such as the 747 can carry 400 passengers, plus the crew, approximately 8,000 km (5,000 miles). On a journey of this length the cabin crew will have the daunting task of providing not just one, but two meals to each of the 400 passengers, in addition to drinks and coffee.

Some of the better airline catering facilities would put even the world's finest hotels to shame. British Airways have a fleet of over 200 aircraft and, in 1978, they out-stripped (or rather out-served) every other world airline by serving 29,000,000 meals to passengers. To achieve this they have £10,000,000 worth of aircraft support equipment based at London Heathrow. Part of this is the new Cabin Services Centre. The new Centre serves as a good example of how efficient and sophisticated airline catering has become. All aspects of British Airways' cabin service are handled from the Centre. Blankets and pillows are supplied for passenger com-

fort, duty-free goods for sale aboard the aircraft, tobacco and drink, toiletries, first aid, magazines, newspapers, flowers, stationery, baby care products, crockery, linen, cutlery, glass and, last but not least, food. These are all items which every airline has to provide and, the more efficient their ground facilities, the easier the task will be for the crew once the aircraft is airborne.

Qantas completed a similar catering facility in 1973. It is one of the most advanced of its kind in the world with the best equipment available, employing 600 staff. The unit works round the clock, 24 hours a day, servicing not only the all-747 Qantas fleet but other airlines as well operating out of Mascot Airport, Sydney. The Flight Catering Centre prepares more than 10,000 meals a day. The bakery produces more than a quarter of a million bread rolls as well as cakes and pastries. A look at the shopping lists gives some idea of just how much food passes through on its way to the passengers. It also gives a fascinating insight into the sheer scale of the whole airline catering operation. Some extracts from British Airways'

and Qantas' annual shopping lists are given on page 113.

The idea of going into a supermarket and buying 30,500 kg (30 tons) of smoked salmon or 150,000 chickens may seem hilarious, but imagine having to cook the 29,000,000 meals that British Airways supplied last year!

## Lobster — by the ton

All food production is under the control of a chief chef and his sous-chefs. British Airways have a repertoire of 20 first-class main dishes at present. These include Cornish lobster in creamed brandy sauce, roast sirloin of Angus beef, chicken with avacado stuffing and quail with truffles — to name just a selection. Concorde passengers are

Right *Preparing food at an airport catering centre.*
Below *Typical galley on the TriStar.*

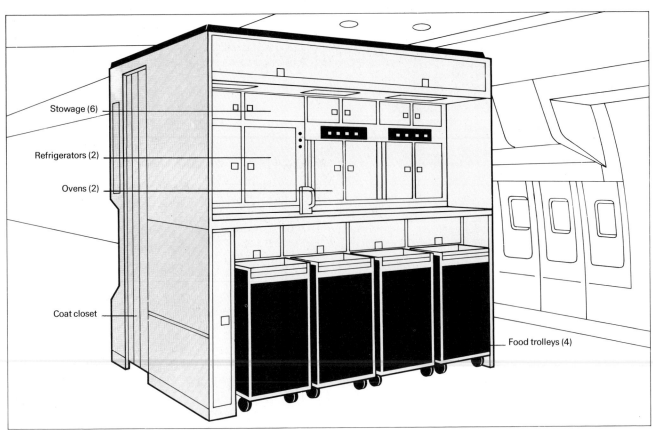

Stowage (6)

Refrigerators (2)

Ovens (2)

Coat closet

Food trolleys (4)

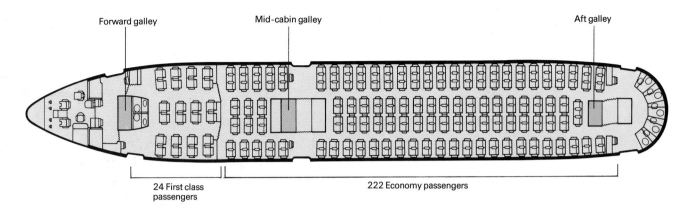

Forward galley          Mid-cabin galley          Aft galley

24 First class
passengers

222 Economy passengers

offered meals from a specially prepared menu. Special food must also be provided for passengers with diabetic or other medical conditions, vegetarians and those whose religion specifies a particular diet. Nearly every kind of special diet is catered for.

Careful planning and high standards of quality, hygiene and presentation are the recipe for success. New menus are discussed at meetings between the executive chef and the management. Special storage areas carry tons of bottles, tins and jars of potential ingredients. The British Airways Services Centre also has a laboratory for carrying out tests on various kinds on food.

Having bought 5,000 kg (5 tons) of prime meat, what do they do with it next? The various dishes are prepared by the chefs — Qantas employs 60 of them — and main courses are partly cooked before being put aboard the aircraft. A giant meal package is put together for each flight and individual dishes are heated up on board. British Airways use 30-second microwave ovens in their aircraft galleys. The cabin

*Seating and galleys aboard an L-1011 TriStar with 24 first class seats.*

crews are trained to handle food and present it well in the confined space available. Huge containers, loaded with every necessity from cutlery to baby food, duty-free goods and first aid, are hoisted up hydraulically to a height of

*Below The Qantas Flight Catering Centre at Sydney's international airport.*

| British Airways | | |
|---|---|---|
| Prime meat | 112,000,000 kg | (110,000 tons) |
| Poultry (portions) | 780,000 | |
| Vegetables (excluding fresh) | 406,500 kg | (400 tons) |
| Smoked salmon | 30,500 kg | (30 tons) |
| Canadian salmon | 73,200 kg | (72 tons) |
| Milk | 2,775,000 litres | (610,500 gal) |
| Butter (pats) | 17,500,000 | |
| | | |
| Qantas | | |
| Bread rolls | 250,000 (approx) | |
| Cooked prawns | 22,000 kg | (20 tons) |
| Chickens | 150,000 | |
| Cream | 160,000 litres | (35,000 gal) |
| Lobster | 14,000 kg | (14 tons) |
| Oysters | 20,000 dozen | |
| Salad | 30,000 cases | |

5.5 m (18 ft), level with the doorway of a 747. By 1980 British Airways will have 36 of these catering hoists in operation.

Once aboard, the meal packages are stowed away until they are needed. Other items are distributed around the aircraft, in the toilets and behind each seat. Duty-free goods such as drink and tobacco are locked away in a special sealed cupboard. Large aircraft have more than one galley – the 747 has five or six, depending on the capacity and layout of the individual aircraft. These are equipped with fast microwave, or much slower air circulation, ovens which can hold up to 28 meals at a time. There are rapid water-boilers and 'hot cupboards' to keep the food warm. To serve up 400 meals there are wheeled trolleys, and special bar trolleys to carry the drinks and snacks. Yet another trolley is reserved for collecting any waste.

When the aircraft returns home all the crockery, linen and waste are hoisted down and any re-usable equipment is returned to be washed. The new British Airways Centre has four huge washing machines which can handle 90,000 pieces of cutlery, 30,000 glasses and 40,000 cups and saucers a day. Everything passes inspection on a conveyor belt before being sorted ready for re-use. Two giant disposal units gobble up all the waste from the aircraft.

Every airline's primary concern is with the safety and comfort of its passengers. The longer the flight, the more likely a passenger is to notice poor service and inferior quality food. Standards have become an important factor in deciding which airline to fly and certain airlines make a great selling-point of the quality of their in-flight catering and entertainment. Apart from the two already mentioned, another airline which prides itself on the high standard of service and catering aboard its aircraft is Singapore Airlines, who now operate a Concorde service to Singapore in conjunction with British Airways.

Not all airlines have their own facilities and many make use of each other's away from their own home airport. There is big business in offering both catering and aircraft maintenance facilities to visiting airlines based in other countries. Standards are such that today a first-class passenger – and in many cases an economy one too – can eat better in the air than on the ground. Good food still tastes good, even 6 miles up at 600 mph!

*Above left Extracts from annual shopping lists for British Airways and Qantas.*
*Left Chefs at the Qantas Flight Catering Centre prepare cold foods under clinically clean conditions for loading aboard an outgoing flight.*

# Crew

Pilot training usually begins at 18. Some airlines have their own training units and may prefer to take on raw recruits before they have had a chance to form any 'bad habits' as private pilots. Once on the flight deck as a co-pilot it can take many years of flying experience before a pilot attains the rank of captain. Captains are usually aged between 40 and 50, on average. They are wholly responsible for the aircraft, the other members of the crew and the passengers aboard. Their word is law, as is that of a ship's captain at sea. The final decision-making lies entirely with the captain and he has the right to refuse a passenger permission to board the aircraft if he feels he is justified.

The amount of experience required to captain an aircraft depends a great deal on the airline and the type of aircraft being flown. It may take 30 years of experience before a captain is given command of a 747 or Concorde. A number of commercial pilots come from military service backgrounds. However experienced they may be at flying Jaguars or Harriers, they will still require retraining before flying a civil aircraft. In fact, civil aircraft vary so much that retraining is usually given before a pilot switches from one civil type to another. A Boeing 737 behaves differently from a TriStar, just as a TriStar behaves differently from a 747. In most cases the layout of the flight deck is slightly different according to the aircraft type, and all these things have to be learned afresh.

Potential recruits are screened for temperament and personality. Obviously the more level-headed and intelligent a potential trainee is, the more likely he or she is to be chosen. Men's fear of women drivers still exists in the aircraft industry, although more women are being accepted for training than ever before. British Airways and Dan-Air are amongst some 15 airlines in the West who employ women pilots but the largest employer of women flight crew is the Russian airline Aeroflot, who have the biggest fleet of civil aircraft in the world.

Training begins on light aircraft, followed by a series of simulator courses which become more and more advanced until the aspiring pilot is actually sitting at the controls of an aircraft in all but reality. The big simulators can recreate every sensation and situation required, simply by programming. The conditions in a simulator are so convincing that even qualified and experienced pilots come out of an 'emergency' situation shaking. A simulator is built to recreate a specific type of aircraft at a cost of several millions. Training is therefore a major investment for an airline with a large fleet of different aircraft. Once they have trained their crew they are obviously keen to keep them on, since they have by then become an investment. Salaries may appear high for airline pilots but it is difficult to assess these when one considers the responsibility pilots carry. The larger the aircraft, the more they are paid.

## In good health

All flight crew from the most senior to the most junior, have to undergo rigorous medical checks at regular intervals. These include ECG testing for heart complaints and tests for hearing and eyesight. A large number of recruits fail to obtain their licences solely on account of poor eyesight. As pilots get older so the medical tests become more stringent and more regular. Fitness is of vital importance if they are to stay in the business of flying aircraft.

A flight crew will fly on average about 700 hours a year. In addition to the captain and his co-pilot there is also a flight engineer who sits on the flight deck behind the other two. He is responsible for the multitude of systems aboard, not only on the flight deck but throughout the whole aircraft. He must make preliminary checks before take-off to see that everything is functioning correctly. He must ensure that the exterior of the aircraft is in a suitable condition to fly. He is responsible to the captain for seeing that all maintenance has been satisfactorily carried out and that the aircraft has been refuelled ready for take off. Once off the ground the flight engineer is constantly monitoring the performance of the engines and

*Ranks among airline personnel.*

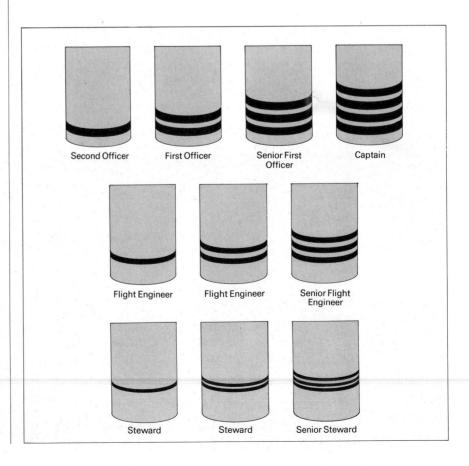

Second Officer    First Officer    Senior First Officer    Captain

Flight Engineer    Flight Engineer    Senior Flight Engineer

Steward    Steward    Senior Steward

feeding vital information to the captain. He can see at a glance any malfunction within or without, whether an electrical fault or a malfunction of the fuel supply system. The role of the flight engineer is too often underrated by the public. He plays a very important part in the flying of an aircraft.

While the flight crew are busy flying the aircraft the cabin crew are equally busy with the passengers. The longer the flight, the more demanding is the task of keeping up to 400 men, women and children fed, entertained and comfortable. An air stewardess, hostess or flight attendant (depending on the airline) has to be a mistress of many trades. Passengers not only require feeding, they become ill, nervous, are sometimes rude or over-keen to make friends. The well-trained stewardess is groomed to cater for all eventualities and to keep a sweet smile on her face however many screaming babies and jolly holidaymakers she may have to cope with.

The cabin crew must be ready to tackle any emergency, quite apart from a failure on the part of the aircraft. Passengers have a knack of picking a 17-hour flight for having heart attacks or producing babies.

Crew receive training from the airline before they begin flying. This covers all aspects of their work, from personal grooming to first aid. They learn the basics of flying and relevant information on the airline that employs them, to enable them to deal with passenger queries. Languages are always a welcome advantage, although the requirements are not as strict as they were years ago when the best stewardesses were always fluent in at least two languages. Some airlines train their staff in passenger psychology and how to handle rude, awkward and obnoxious individuals calmly and efficiently. They are also taught to deal with nervous and first-time fliers.

## The perfect hostess

Meals are pre-packed and only need re-heating, usually in microwave ovens. Even so, there are still a lot of meals to serve and it takes practice to weave your way down the aisle of a packed 747 wielding a trolley full of lamb cutlets or Campari sodas. Drinks, magazines, newspapers and duty-free goods must all be served and the money collected. Help must be given to disabled passengers, nursing mothers and the elderly. A well-qualified cabin attendant is a combined nurse, waitress, social worker and hostess all rolled into one and their behaviour is a reflection on the airline.

In the event of an emergency a great deal of initiative and self-control is required on the part of all cabin crew calmly and quickly to evacuate several hundred passengers in a few minutes, knowing all the time that they, the cabin crew, will be the last to leave. Fire is always a major threat and even if the aircraft has managed to land safely there is still a danger of fire breaking out, particularly if the undercarriage has failed to lower.

Training takes place in a mock-up cabin. Some airlines use an old aircraft no longer in service to train the crew in how to move quickly and efficiently with loads of meals and drinks. Swimming pools are used for evacuation training in the use of life rafts. Trainees are shown how to use life jackets and inflatable rafts and they are given lessons in artificial respiration.

To the passenger the cabin crew should always appear smiling, relaxed, helpful and confident – and this is probably their most demanding task of all.

*Simulators play a vital role in the training programme of all flight crew. They are not only useful for initial training but for retraining experienced pilots on new or unfamiliar types of aircraft. Here a 747 approaches the 'runway' at an 'altitude' of 1,500 ft.*

# Civil Aircraft

### Airbus Industrie A300/A310     International

| | |
|---|---|
| Data: | A300B2-100 |
| Span: | 44.8 m (147 ft 1 in) |
| Length: | 53.6 m (175 ft 11 in) |
| Gross weight: | 142,000 kg (313,060 lb) |
| Payload: | 34,580 kg (76,240 lb) |
| Range: | 3,400 km (2,100 miles) |
| Cruise speed: | 869 km/h (540 mph) |
| Accommodation: | 241/345 |
| Power unit: | 2 × 23,130 kg (51,000 lb) st General Electric CF6-50C turbofans |

Operators include: **A300** Air France, Eastern, Iran Air, Laker, Lufthansa, Olympic, SAS; **A310** Air France, Eastern, Iberia, Lufthansa, Swissair

### BAC One-Eleven     UK

| | |
|---|---|
| Data: | One-Eleven 500 |
| Span: | 28.4 m (93 ft) |
| Length: | 24.6 m (80 ft 8 in) |
| Gross weight: | 19,958 kg (44,000 lb) |
| Payload: | 11,760 kg (25,933 lb) |
| Range: | 2,301 km (1,430 miles) |
| Cruise speed: | 847 km (526 mph) |
| Accommodation: | 119 |
| Power unit: | 2 × 5,700 kg (12,550 lb) st Rolls-Royce Spey 512-14DW turbofans |

Operators include: Aer Lingus, Air Malawi, Air Pacific, American Airlines, Braniff, British Airways, British Caledonian, British Eagle, Gulf, Laker, Phillpines Airlines, Sultan of Oman's Air Force, Tarom

### Boeing 707     USA

| | |
|---|---|
| Data: | 707-320C |
| Span: | 44.4 m (145 ft 9 in) |
| Length: | 46.6 m (152 ft 9 in) |
| Gross weight: | 151,300 kg (333,600 lb) |
| Payload: | 24,450 kg (53,900 lb) |
| Range: | 5,300 km (3,300 miles) |
| Cruise speed: | 885 km/h (550 mph) |
| Accommodation: | 100/159 |
| Power unit: | 4 × 8,600 kg (19,000 lb) st Pratt & Whitney JT3D-7A two-spool turbofans |

Operators include: Aerolineas Argentinas, Air France, Air-India, American Airways, Avianca, Braniff, British Airways, British Caledonian, China Air Lines, El Al, Flying Tiger, Iran Air, Iraqi Airways, Lufthansa, Olympic, Pan American, Qantas, Sabena, Saudia, Seaboard, South African Airways, Sudan, Tarom, Trans World, USAF, Varig, Wardair

## Boeing 727                                 USA

| | |
|---|---|
| **Data:** | 727-200 |
| **Span:** | 32.9 m (108 ft) |
| **Length:** | 46.7 m (153 ft 2 in) |
| **Gross weight:** | 95,000 kg (209,500 lb) |
| **Payload:** | 18,600 kg (41,000 lb) |
| **Range:** | 2,540 km (1,580 miles) |
| **Cruise speed:** | 883 km/h (549 mph) |
| **Accommodation:** | 189 |
| **Power unit:** | 3 × 7,250 kg (16,000 lb) st Pratt & Whitney JT8D-17 turbofans |

Operators include: Aerolineas Argentinas, Air Algerie, Air Canada, Air France, Air Jamaica, Alia, Alitalia, Allegheny, All Nippon, American, Avianca, Braniff, China Air Lines, Delta, Eastern, Iberia, Iran Air, Iraqi Airways, Libyan Arab, Lufthansa, Mexicana, National, Olympic, Pan American, Sabena, Singapore Airlines, TAP, Trans World, United, Western

## Boeing 737                                 USA

| | |
|---|---|
| **Data:** | 737-200 |
| **Span:** | 28.35 m (93 ft) |
| **Length:** | 30.5 m (100 ft) |
| **Gross weight:** | 53,000 kg (117,000 lb) |
| **Payload:** | 15,400 kg (34,000 lb) |
| **Range:** | 2,540 km (1,580 miles) |
| **Cruise speed:** | 808 km/h (502 mph) |
| **Accommodation:** | 130 |
| **Power unit:** | 2 × 7,250 kg (16,000 lb) st Pratt & Witney JT8D-17 turbofans |

Operators include: Aer Lingus, Aerolineas Argentinas, Air Algerie, Air Gabon, Air Liberia, Air Madagascar, Air Tanzania, Air Zaïre, All Nippon, Avianca, Britannia, British Airways, Delta, Egyptair, Gulf Air, Iran Air, Iraqi Airways, Kuwait, Lufthansa, Nordair, Olympic, Orion, Pacific Southwest, Pacific Western, Sabena, Saudia, Transair Canada, Transavia, United, USAF, Varig, Western

## Boeing 747                                 USA

| | |
|---|---|
| **Data:** | 747-200B |
| **Span:** | 59,6 m (195 ft 8 in) |
| **Length:** | 70.5 m (231 ft 4 in) |
| **Gross weight:** | 356,100 kg (785,000 lb) |
| **Payload:** | 71,500 kg (157,700 lb) |
| **Range:** | 8,850 km (5,500 miles) |
| **Cruise speed:** | 907 km/h (564 mph) |
| **Accommodation:** | 395/400 |
| **Power unit options:** | 4 × 24,000 kg (53,000 lb) st Pratt & Whitney JT9D-7Q turbofans |
| | 4 × 23,800 kg (52,500 lb) st General Electric CF6-50E2 turbofans |
| | 4 × 23,100 kg (51,000 lb) st Rolls-Royce RB211-524B turbofans |

Operators include: Aer Lingus, Air Canada, Air France, Air-India, Alia, Alitalia, Avianca, American, Braniff, British Airways, China Air Lines, Delta, Eastern, El Al, Iberia, Iran Air, JAL, KLM, Kuwait, Lufthansa, MEA, Olympic, Pan Am, Qantas, SAA, Sabena, SAS, Swissair, TAP, United Wardair

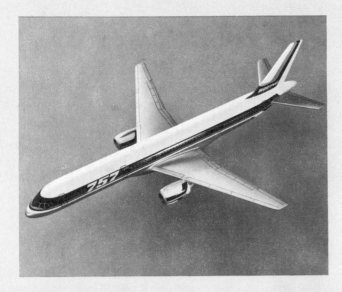

## Boeing 757 USA

| | |
|---|---|
| **Gross weight:** | 99,800 kg (220,000 lb) (basic)<br>104,300 kg (230,000 lb) |
| **Range:** | 3,650–4,520 km (2,268–2,809 miles)<br>with Rolls-Royce engines<br>3,761–4,651 km (2,337–2,890 miles)<br>with General Electric engines |
| **Accommodation:** | 178/229 (basic) 180/230 |
| **Power unit options:** | 2 × 16,900 kg (37,300 lb) st<br>Rolls-Royce RB211-535 turbofans<br>2 × 16,500 kg (36,330 lb) st General<br>Electric CF6-32 turbofans |

Orders (with R-R RB211 engines): British Airways (19),
Eastern (21)

## Boeing 767 USA

The first 767s are scheduled for delivery in mid-1982. An
order for 30 767-200s powered by Pratt & Whitney
JT9D-7R turbofans has been placed by United Airlines. The
engine, which is rated at just over 20,000 kg (44,000 lb)
thrust was chosen in preference to the alternative General
Electric CF6-80A. The 767-200 will seat 200/210
passengers. It has a payload of over 18,000 kg (40,000 lb)
over a range of approximately 4,500 km (2,800 miles).
International Lease Finance have ordered ten 767s and
Trans World have ten due for delivery in 1982 and an option
for ten more.

## British Aerospace/Aérospatiale Concorde UK/France

| | |
|---|---|
| **Span:** | 25.6 m (83 ft 10 in) |
| **Length:** | 62.1 m (203 ft 9 in) |
| **Gross weight:** | 185,000 kg (408,000 lb) |
| **Payload:** | 11,500 kg (25,000 lb) |
| **Range:** | 6,100 km (3,800 miles) |
| **Cruise speed:** | 2,124 km/h (1,320 mph) |
| **Accommodation:** | 100/128 |
| **Power unit:** | 4 × 17,260 kg (38,050 lb) st<br>Rolls-Royce Bristol/SNECMA Olympus<br>593 two-spool turbojets |

Operators: Air France, British Airways, Braniff (in
conjunction with British Airways), Singapore Airways (in
conjunction with British Airways)

## British Aerospace (HS) 748     UK

| | |
|---|---|
| **Data:** | Series 2B |
| **Span:** | 31.24 m (102 ft 6 in) |
| **Length:** | 20.42 m (67 ft) |
| **Gross weight:** | 21,100 kg (46,500 lb) |
| **Payload:** | 5,700 kg (12,500 lb) |
| **Range:** | 1,770 km (1,100 miles) |
| **Cruise speed:** | 448 km/h (278 mph) |
| **Accommodation:** | 40/56 |
| **Power unit:** | 2 × 2,280 eshp Rolls-Royce Dart R.Da.7 Mk 536-2 turboprops |

Operators include: Aerolineas Argentinas, Air Ceylon, Air Liberia, Austrian Airlines, Avianca, Bahamas Airways, Belgian Air Force, Brazilian Air Force, Channel Airways, Indian Air Force, Korean Air Force, South African Airways, Transair Canada

## Fokker-VFW International F27 Friendship     Netherlands

| | |
|---|---|
| **Data:** | F27 Friendship Series 500 |
| **Span:** | 29 m (95 ft 2 in) |
| **Length:** | 25.1 m (82 ft 3 in) |
| **Gross weight:** | 20,500 kg (45,000 lb) |
| **Payload:** | 5,970 kg (13,160 lb) |
| **Range:** | 1,741 km (1,082 miles) |
| **Cruise speed:** | 480 km/h (298 mph) |
| **Accommodation:** | 40/56 |
| **Power unit:** | 2 × 2,140 shp Rolls-Royce Dart R.Da.7 Mk 532-7R turboprops |

Operators include: Aer Lingus, Air Algerie, Air Inter, Air France, Alia, Algeria, All Nippon, Bangladesh Biman, Burma Airways, Indian Airlines, Korean Airways, Malaysia-Singapore Airlines, Nigeria Airways, Pakistan International Airlines, Swissair, Trans-Australia Airlines

## Fokker-VFW International F28 Fellowship     Netherlands

| | |
|---|---|
| **Data:** | F28 Mk 6000 |
| **Span:** | 25.07 m (82 ft 3 in) |
| **Length:** | 29.6 m (97 ft 1 in) |
| **Gross weight:** | 30,200 kg (66,500 lb) |
| **Payload:** | 9,555 kg (21,065 lb) |
| **Range:** | 1,650 km (1,025 miles) |
| **Cruise speed:** | 850 km/h (528 mph) |
| **Accommodation:** | 85 |
| **Power unit:** | 2 × 4,500 kg (9,850 lb) st Rolls-Royce Spey Mk 555-15H turbofans |

Operators include: Aerolineas Argentinas, AeroPeru, Air Gabon, Ansett, Bavaria Germanair, Braathens SAFE, Iberia, Nigeria Airways, Ghana Airways, Air Anglia, Royal Swazi

## Hawker Siddeley Trident      UK

| | |
|---|---|
| **Data:** | Trident 2E |
| **Span:** | 29.87 m (98 ft) |
| **Length:** | 34.97 m (114 ft 9 in) |
| **Gross weight:** | 65,300 kg (144,000 lb) |
| **Payload:** | 13,400 kg (29,600 lb) |
| **Range:** | 3,965 km (2,464 miles) |
| **Cruise speed:** | 960 km/h (596 mph) |
| **Accommodation:** | 128-180 |
| **Power unit:** | 3 × 5,425 kg (11,960 lb) st Roll-Royce Spey Mk 512-5W turbofans |

Operators include: British Airways, CAAC

## Ilyushin Il-62      USSR

| | |
|---|---|
| **Span:** | 43.06 m (141 ft 3½ in) |
| **Length:** | 53.08 m (174 ft 2 in) |
| **Gross weight:** | 157,639 kg (347,224 lb) |
| **Payload:** | 23,000 kg (50,706 lb) |
| **Range:** | 9,200 km (5,716 miles) |
| **Cruise speed:** | 849 km/h (528 mph) |
| **Accommodation:** | 186 |
| **Power unit:** | 4 × 11,500 kg (25,350 lb) st Soloviev D-30KU turbofans |

Operators include: Aeroflot, CAAC, CSA, Interflug, LOT, Tarom

## Ilyushin Il-76      USSR

| | |
|---|---|
| **Data:** | Medium/long-range freighter |
| **Span:** | 50.50 m (165 ft 8 in) |
| **Length:** | 46.59 m (152 ft 10½ in) |
| **Gross weight:** | 157,000 kg (346,125 lb) |
| **Payload:** | 40,000 kg (88,185 lb) |
| **Range:** | 5,000 km (3,100 miles) |
| **Cruise speed:** | 850 km/h (528 mph) |
| **Accommodation:** | Flight crew of 3 |
| **Power unit:** | 4 × 12,000 kg (26,500 lb) st Soloviev D-30KP turbofans |

Operators include: Aeroflot, Soviet Air Force

### Lockheed L-1011 TriStar  USA

| | |
|---|---|
| **Data:** | L-1011-200 |
| **Span:** | 47.34 m (155 ft 4 in) |
| **Length:** | 54.15 m (177 ft 8 in) |
| **Gross weight:** | 202,300 kg (446,000 lb) |
| **Payload:** | 33,700 kg (74,200 lb) |
| **Range:** | 7,870 km (4,890 miles) |
| **Cruise speed:** | 913 km/h (567 mph) |
| **Accommodation:** | 256/400 |
| **Power unit:** | 3 × 21,750 kg (48,000 lb) st Rolls-Royce RB211-524 three-spool turbofans |

Operators include: AeroPeru, Air Canada, British Airways, BWIA, Cathay Pacific, Delta, Eastern, Gulf Air, Haas-Turner, LTU, PSA, Pan American, Saudi, Trans World

### McDonnell Douglas DC-8  USA

| | |
|---|---|
| **Data:** | Super Sixty Series |
| **Span:** | 45.23 m (148 ft 5 in) |
| **Length:** | 57.12 m (187 ft 5 in) |
| **Gross weight:** | 158,760 kg (350,000 lb) |
| **Payload:** | 30,724 kg (67,735 lb) |
| **Range:** | 5,650 km (3,500 miles) |
| **Cruise speed:** | 965 km/h (600 mph) |
| **Accommodation:** | 259 |
| **Power unit:** | 4 × 8,600 kg (19,000 lb) st Pratt & Whitney JT3D-7 turbofans |

Operators include: Air Canada, Air Gabon, Air Jamaica, Alitalia, Braniff, Flying Tiger, Eastern, Finnair, Iberia, JAL, KLM, National, SAS, Scanair, Seaboard, Swissair, Trans International, United

### McDonnell Douglas DC-9  USA

| | |
|---|---|
| **Data:** | DC-9 Super 80 |
| **Span:** | 32.9 m (107 ft 10 in) |
| **Length:** | 45.06 m (147 ft 10 in) |
| **Gross weight:** | 63,500 kg (140,000 lb) |
| **Payload:** | 17,842 kg (39,334 lb) |
| **Range:** | 2,427 km (1,508 miles) |
| **Cruise speed:** | 840 km/h (522 mph) |
| **Accommodation:** | 172 |
| **Power unit:** | 2 × 8,750 kg (19,250 lb) st Pratt & Whitney JT8D-209 turbofans |

Operators include: Aeromexico, Air California, Air Canada, Air Jamaica, Alitalia, Allegheny, Ansettt, Delta, Eastern, Iberia, KLM, Saudia, Swissair, Trans World

## McDonnell Douglas DC-10      USA

| | |
|---|---|
| **Data:** | DC-10-40 |
| **Span:** | 50.39 m (165 ft 4 in) |
| **Length:** | 55.55 m (182 ft 3 in) |
| **Gross weight:** | 259,450 kg (572,000 lb) |
| **Payload:** | 46,237 kg (101,935 lb) |
| **Range:** | 9,395 km (5,838 miles) |
| **Cruise speed:** | 925 km/h (574 mph) |
| **Accommodation:** | 380 |
| **Power unit:** | 3 × 24,000 kg (53,000 lb) st Pratt & Whitney JT9D-59A two-spool turbofans |

Operators include: Aeromexico, Air Afrique, Air New Zealand, Air Zaïre, Alitalia, Balair, British Caledonian, Condor, CP Air, Finnair, Garuda, Iberia, JAT, KLM, Korean Air Lines, Laker, Lufthansa, National, Nigeria, Pakistan International, Philippine Airlines, SAS, Singapore Airlines, Swissair, Thai, UTA, Varig, Wardair

## Tupolev Tu-134      USSR

| | |
|---|---|
| **Data:** | Tu-134A |
| **Span:** | 29 m (95 ft 2 in) |
| **Length:** | 37.19 m (122 ft) |
| **Gross weight:** | 47,000 kg (103,600 lb) |
| **Payload:** | 8,200 kg (18,000 lb) |
| **Range:** | 2,000 km (1,250 miles) |
| **Cruise speed:** | 750-900 km/h (465-560 mph) |
| **Accommodation:** | 80 |
| **Power unit:** | 2 × 6,800 kg (15,000 lb) st Soloviev D-30-2 turbofans |

Operators include: Aeroflot, Balkan Bulgarian, CSA, Interflug, LOT, Malev

## Tupolev TU-144      USSR

| | |
|---|---|
| **Span:** | 28.80 m (94 ft 6 in) |
| **Length:** | 65.70 m (215 ft 6½ in) |
| **Gross weight:** | 180,000 kg (397,000 lb) |
| **Range:** | 6,500 km (4,000 miles) |
| **Cruise speed:** | Mach 2.2 (2,336 km/h (1,452 mph)) at 16,000–18,000 m (52,500–59,000 ft) |
| **Power unit:** | 4 × 20,000 kg (44,000 lb) st (plus afterburning) Kuznetsov NK-144 turbofans |

The second production TU-144 was lost while demonstrating at the Paris Air Show in 1973. Although three more examples were in service by 1975 they were only used for cargo transport and the type was finally 'suspended'. Rumours that services are to be resumed are, as yet, unconfirmed but the Soviet Union has announced that design improvements are being incorporated in a new TU-144D which will have a 50% reduction in fuel consumption and extended range capability of 7,000 km (4,350 miles).

## Tupolev Tu-154     USSR

| | |
|---|---|
| **Data:** | Tu-154A |
| **Span:** | 37.55 m (123 ft 2½ in) |
| **Length:** | 47.90 m (157 ft 1¾ in) |
| **Gross weight:** | 90,000 kg (196,500 lb) |
| **Payload:** | 20,000 kg (44,000 lb) |
| **Range:** | 3,800 km (2,360 miles) |
| **Cruise speed:** | 850-975 km/h (528-605 mph) |
| **Accommodation:** | 167 |
| **Power unit:** | 3 × 9,500 kg (21,000 lb) st Kuznetsov NK-8-2 turbofans |

Operators include: Aeroflot, Balkan Bulgarian, Malev

## Vickers VC-10     UK

| | |
|---|---|
| **Data:** | Super VC-10 |
| **Span:** | 44.55 m (146 ft 2 in) |
| **Length:** | 52.32 m (171 ft 8 in) |
| **Gross weight:** | 151,950 kg (335,000 lb) |
| **Payload:** | 18,325 kg (40,400 lb) |
| **Range:** | 7,450 km (4,630 miles) |
| **Cruise speed:** | 914 km/h (568 mph) |
| **Accommodation:** | 174 |
| **Power unit:** | 4 × 10,200 kg (22,500 lb) st Rolls-Royce Conway 550 turbofans |

Operators include: British Airways, Royal Air Force

## Vickers Viscount     UK

| | |
|---|---|
| **Span:** | 28.56 m (93 ft 8½ in) |
| **Length:** | 26.11 m (85 ft 8 in) |
| **Gross weight:** | 32,900 kg (72,500 lb) |
| **Payload:** | 6,600 kg (14,500 lb) |
| **Range:** | 2,830 km (1,760 miles) |
| **Cruise speed:** | 576 km/h (358 mph) |
| **Accommodation:** | 52/75 |
| **Power unit:** | 4 × 1,990 eph Rolls-Royce Dart 525 turboprop |

Operators include: British Airways, British Midland Airways

# Glossary

**Accelerometer** — instrument for measuring increases in speed.

**Acrophobia** — terror of heights.

**Aileron** — movable control surface on the trailing edge of an aircraft's wing.

**Air traffic control (ATC)** — operation responsible for directing aircraft movements in the air.

**Airbridge** — covered walkway connecting terminal departure area and aircraft for passenger embarkation.

**Aircraft surface movement indicator (ASMI)** — panel in the control tower upon which all ground movements can be monitored.

**Airfoil** — structure, such as a wing, designed to generate lift when propelled forwards through the air.

**Airspeed indicator (ASI)** — instrument indicating the aircraft's speed in knots and Mach number.

**Altimeter** — instrument indicating the altitude at which an aircraft is flying.

**Altitude** — height, usually above sea-level.

**Attitude director** — instrument indicating the pitch and roll movements of an aircraft relative to the earth's horizon.

**Annular duct** — ring-shaped air duct in a jet engine.

**Approach speed** — speed at which an aircraft makes its final landing approach.

**Artificial horizon** — a gyro-stabilized instrument on the flight deck showing the pitching and rolling movements of the aircraft.

**Automatic landing (autoland)** — system enabling an aircraft to land independently of the pilot's manual control using an ILS.

**Automatic pilot (autopilot)** — gyroscopically controlled device capable of controlling and directing the aircraft according to pre-set instructions.

**Batsman** — sometimes called a marshaller, a person who directs an aircraft into a parking bay using circular 'bats' to indicate his instructions.

**Bearing** — relative position.

**Beacon** — radio transmitter emitting regular signals for use in navigation.

**Bucket** — or clamshell, movable shell-shaped deflectors round the exhaust nozzle of a jet engine for achieving reverse thrust when activated from the flight deck.

**Burn rate** — rate at which fuel is consumed.

**By-pass engine** — jet engine in which a proportion of the intake air is ducted round rather than through the combustion chamber.

**Call sign** — designation by which a pilot identifies his aircraft to traffic control.

**Catering hoist** — vehicle carrying a container of ready-prepared meals, drink, linen or other equipment, which can be raised on a scissor-lift to the height of the aircraft's door for loading.

**Chord** — distance from the leading to the trailing edge of an airfoil.

**Clamshell** — see 'bucket'.

**Clear air turbulence (CAT)** — type of turbulence not detectable on a weather radar screen.

**Cockpit voice recorder (CVR)** — equipment which makes a continuous recording of all conversation on the flight deck, the last 30 minutes of which is always retained.

**Combustion chamber** — part of a jet engine where air and jet fuel combust to form high-temperature gases which are then expelled through the exhaust system to achieve thrust.

**Compressor** — part of any aircraft engine where the density of intake air is increased by compression.

**Control tower** — elevated position with a clear view of the airport concourse and runways, housing staff in charge of vehicle and aircraft ground movements, take-off and final approach.

**Convergent nozzle** — referring to the exhaust system of a jet engine, where the nozzle converges to form a small outlet thereby increasing the pressure of the exhaust gases and the thrust they produce.

**Cruise speed** — speed calculated to give maximum efficiency and low fuel consumption over a long distance.

**Decision speed** — point at which a pilot must decide whether or not to go ahead with take-off.

**Delta wing** — triangular wing section of the type used on Concorde and the TU-144, developed specifically for supersonic flight. Other examples exist on military aircraft such as the Vulcan bomber and the Saab Viggen short take-off (STOL) fighter.

**Doppler** — airborne radar equipment which determines the position and speed of the aircraft carrying it by measuring changes in frequency in beams transmitted and reflected back to it from the ground.

**Drag** — resistance of air to a moving object.

**Duty-free** — goods which can be purchased free of tax or duty normally imposed.

**Elevation** — height above sea-level.

**Elevator** — movable control surface on the horizontal stabilizer of an aircraft (see also 'elevon').

**Elevon** — wing-mounted control surface combining the functions of both elevator and aileron.

**Flap** — movable control surface on the wing trailing edge for increasing lift.

**Flight recorder** — device which records the height, speed, position and other important details of a flight for use in the event of an incident. The container is crash-proof and is usually fitted with an under-water recovery beacon.

**'Follow me'** — vehicle bearing the instruction 'follow me' for guiding pilots from one part of the airport to another.

**Fuel farm** — underground fuel storage installation.

**Galley** — area where food is prepared aboard an aircraft.

**Glidepath** — vertical beam from the glide slope transmitter which combines with the horizontal beam from the localizer of an ILS.

**'Go around'** — term used when a pilot decides to abandon a landing attempt and try again.

**Ground control** — operation in charge of vehicle and aircraft movements on the ground.

**Gyroscope** — a rotating wheel mounted in a ring, having its axis free to turn in any direction.

**Head-up display (HUD)** — information projected on to the windshield of an aircraft enabling the pilot to read it without lowering his eyes to the instrument panel.

**Hold** — to maintain a given position and altitude over a beacon until permission is granted for the aircraft to make its landing approach.

| | |
|---|---|
| **Holding point** | position, usually over a beacon, where ATC will instruct an aircraft to circle until there is airspace for it to continue its journey. |
| **Horizontal stabilizer** | horizontal airfoil on the tail of an aircraft, usually either pivoted or incorporating adjustable control surfaces (elevators). (Concorde has no horizontal stabilizer.) |
| **Inertial navigation system (INS)** | system comprising three accelerometers which continuously measure changes in speed and direction, from which information the aircraft's position is calculated by computer. |
| **Instrument landing system (ILS)** | two radio beams which combine to form an invisible sloping path and which can be followed by the pilot when landing for a perfect descent and touchdown. |
| **Lift** | force which supports an aircraft when airborne. |
| **Localizer** | transmitter which puts out an angled horizontal beam along a straight line of approach to the runway. When combined with the vertical sloping beam of the glideslope transmitter, these beams can be used as an approach guide for incoming aircraft. |
| **Mach number** | indication of the ratio of true airspeed to the local speed of sound, varying according to altitude. |
| **Navaids** | navigational aids. |
| **Navigation** | methods of determining an aircraft's position and course. |
| **Omega system** | new navigation system consisting of eight transmitters positioned around the world, each emitting a synchronized signal for interpretation by the aircraft's computer. |
| **Outer marker** | first beacon an aircraft must locate on approach to an airport. |
| **Overshoot** | to touchdown beyond the ideal touchdown zone, possibly causing the aircraft to leave the end of the runway. |
| **Pitch** | up/down motion of the aircraft's nose; also refers to the proximity of rows of seating aboard an aircraft. |
| **Port** | left side. |
| **Push-back** | term used by pilots when requesting to be towed out of a parking bay. |
| **Pylon** | vertical strut on the underside of a wing to which an engine is attached. |
| **Rapid intervention vehicle (RIV)** | emergency fire tender capable of moving over rough terrain at high speed. |
| **Reheat** | or afterburner; system in which exhaust gas is re-used by injecting and igniting fuel to give extra thrust for supersonic aircraft. |
| **Reverse thrust** | to deflect the thrust of a jet engine forwards causing a braking effect. |
| **Roll** | up/down movement of an aircraft's wingtips as it rotates about the longitudinal axis from nose to tail. |
| **Rotate** | to raise the nose of an aircraft at the moment of take-off. |
| **Rudder** | control surface in the vertical stabilizer controlling the yaw of an aircraft. |
| **Slat** | auxiliary wing section positioned on the leading edge of an airfoil to increase lift. |
| **Spill door** | small flap which opens inwards to serve as an auxiliary air inlet on a jet engine. |
| **Spoiler** | control surface on an aircraft's wing to reduce lift by impeding the flow of air. |
| **Spool** | alternative term for the compressor section of a jet engine. |
| **Stack** | term used to describe a number of aircraft at different altitudes circling at a holding point. |
| **Stall** | loss of lift due to an excessive angle of attack or insufficient speed. |

| | |
|---|---|
| **Starboard** | right side. |
| **Stick-pusher** | safety device which automatically forces the control column forward to recover an aircraft from stall if the pilot fails to act on the warning given by the stick-shaker. |
| **Stick-shaker** | warning device which causes the control column to shake if an aircraft is approaching a stall. |
| **Strobe** | (from stroboscope) a fast-flashing light such as those positioned on the wingtips and fuselage of an aircraft. |
| **Super foam tender** | large-capacity foam carrier for preventing or extinguishing fire in an emergency situation. |
| **Supersonic** | in excess of the speed of sound. |
| **Taxi** | of aircraft, to move forward on the ground at very low speed. |
| **Taxiway** | interconnecting access routes to and from terminals and runways for aircraft movement. |
| **Throttle** | control by which engine thrust can be increased or diminished. |
| **Thrust** | force emitted by a jet engine which impels it and the aircraft forward. |
| **Trailing edge** | rear edge of wing or airfoil. |
| **Turbofan** | jet engine in which most of the intake air passes through a large fan and then by-passes the combustion chamber. |
| **Turbulence** | disrupted and irregular flow of air. |
| **Turbojet** | jet engine in which all the intake air passes through the combustion chamber, (also called a pure jet). |
| **Turboprop** | turbine engine which drives a front-mounted propeller. |
| **Undershoot** | to touchdown too soon, before the threshold of the runway. |
| **Variable geometry** | where the shape or position of the component parts can be altered as in variable geometry intake and exhaust systems. |
| **Velocity-one ($V_1$)** | point after which a pilot must proceed with take-off. |
| **Velocity-rotate ($V_R$)** | point at which the aircraft rotates on take-off. |
| **Vertical stabilizer** | vertical tail section of an aircraft incorporating the rudder. |
| **VOR** | Very high frequency Omni-directional Range; a system of radio transmitters used in navigation whose signals can be received by instruments aboard the aircraft. |
| **Visual approach slope indicator (VASI)** | framework containing red and white lights which, viewed by the pilot through slats, indicate whether he is approaching to land at the correct angle. |

**Standard Abbreviations**

| | |
|---|---|
| **ADF** | Automatic Direction Finding |
| **ASI** | Airspeed Indicator |
| **ASMI** | Aircraft Surface Movement Indicator |
| **ATCC** | Air Traffic Control Centre |
| **CAT** | Clear Air Turbulence |
| **CVR** | Cockpit Voice Recorder |
| **HUD** | Head-Up Display |
| **ILS** | Instrument Landing System |
| **INS** | Inertial Navigation System |
| **OBS** | Omni Bearing Selector |
| **RIV** | Rapid Intervention Vehicle |
| **SBA** | Standard Beam Approach |
| **SST** | Supersonic Transport Aircraft |
| **STOL** | Short Take-Off or Landing |
| **VASI** | Visual Approach Slope Indicator |
| **VOR** | VHF Omni-directional Range |
| **$V_1$** | Velocity-One |
| **$V_R$** | Velocity-Rotate |

# Index

## A

Abu Dhabi Airport 21
Accident rate 96
Accidents *see* Emergencies
ADF (Automatic Direction
  Finding) 67
Aeroflot 114
Ailerons 72, 82
Air France 17, 18
Air stewardesses 115
Air traffic control centres (ATCC)
  54, 55, 57
Air traffic controllers 57, 75, 76
Airbus Industrie A300/A310 116
Aircraft engine configurations
  101
Aircraft engine failure 75
Aircraft engines 37, 100
  Concorde 105
Aircraft interiors 108
Aircraft types *see* under name
  of manufacturer
Aircraft weight 50, 108
Airport emergency services 42
Airport medical services 12
Airport observation decks 23
Airport passenger services 23
Airport terminal buildings 22
Airport vehicles 32
Airports *see* under name of city
Airspeed 86
Alitalia 20
Altitude 76, 95
Amsterdam Schipol Airport 18,
  57
Automatic landing 80

## B

BAC One-Eleven 38, 116
Baggage 26, 37
Batsmen 55
Boeing 707 45, 91, 116
Boeing 727 117
Boeing 737 117
Boeing 747 117
  cargo 45
  flight deck 82
  fuel 38
  landing 77
  passengers 109
  take off 75
  weight 50
Boeing 757 118
Boeing 767 118
British Aerospace 748 119
British Aerospace/Aérospatiale
  Concorde 104, 118
  aircraft engines 105

altitude 95
delta wing 90
flight controls 73
flight deck 86
fuel economy 38
fuel transfer 41
British Airways 110, 112

## C

Call signs 55, 75
Captain *see* Pilot
Cargo 37, 44, 45
Cargo handling 45
Cathay Pacific Airways 20
Certificate of Airworthiness 90,
  96
Chicago O'Hare Airport 11, 16,
  41, 50
Clear air turbulence (CAT) 94
Climb 75
Closed circuit television 27
Clouds 88
Cockpit voice recorder (CVR) 87
Computers 57, 69, 74
  cargo handling 45
Concorde *see* British
  Aerospace/Aérospatiale
  Concorde
Containers (cargo) 44
Control surfaces 72
Co-pilots 114
Crash recorder 87
Crew training 115
Customs officers 26

## D

Dallas-Fort Worth Airport 10,
  16, 50
Delta wing 73, 90
Departures 27
Doppler navigation system 67
Dubai Airport 21
Duty-free shops 23

## E

Elevators (control surfaces) 72,
  73
Elevons 73
Emergencies 42, 78
Emergency packs 94
Emergency services 42

## F

Fail safe 91
Fire fighting 42, 43
First class 109
Flight controls 72, 73
Flight crew 114
Flight deck 82, 86
Flight engineer 114
Flight numbers 55
Fokker VFW International F27
  Friendship 119
Fokker VFW International F28
  Fellowship 119
Frankfurt Rhein/Main Airport 19,
  45
Fuel consumption 38
Fuel economy 38, 40
Fuel farms 35, 38
Fuel hazards 42
Fuel storage 38, 41
Fuel tanks (aircraft) 40, 41
Fuel transfer 40, 41, 106

## G

General Electric (engines) 101
Ground controller 55

## H

Hawker-Siddeley 125 78
Hawker-Siddeley Comet 91
Hawker-Siddeley Trident 80,
  120
Holding point 55, 76
Hong Kong Kai Tak Airport 11,
  20, 50

## I

Ilyushin IL-62 120
Ilyushin IL-76 120
Immigration officers 26
Inertial Navigation System (INS)
  68
Instrument Landing System
  (ILS) 55, 58, 60, 76
Instruments 86
International Civil Aviation
  Organisation (ICAO) 11

## J

JAL (Japanese Air Lines) 21
Jet engines 100, 105

## K

KLM Royal Dutch Airlines 19

## L

Landing 42, 55, 76, 77, 80
Life jackets 94
Lockheed L-1011 TriStar 45 121
London Gatwick Airport 17, 20,
    24
London Heathrow Airport 11, 17
    air traffic control 54, 57
    automatic landing 80
    fuel supplies 41
    passenger catering 110
    runways 50, 51
Lufthansa 17, 19

## M

McDonnell Douglas DC-8 121
McDonnell Douglas DC-9 78,
    88, 121
McDonnell Douglas DC-10 91,
    121
Mail 45
Maintenance 37, 90
Manchester Ringway Airport 50
Metal fatigue 90
Metals 104, 105
Milan Linate Airport 50

## N

Navaids (navigational aids) 62
Navigation 62, 88
New York John F. Kennedy
    Airport 11, 14, 16
    cargo handling 45
    fuel farm 35, 38
    runways 50

## O

Omega navigation system 68

## P

Pan Am (Pan American World
    Airways) 17
Paris Charles de Gaulle Airport 18

Paris Orly Airport 18
Passenger catering 23, 35, 110
Passenger check-in 22, 26, 27
Passenger comfort 108, 113
Passenger flow 26
Passenger insurance 23
Passenger seats 109
Passenger services 23
Pilot training 114
Pilots 54, 55, 62, 74, 77, 82
Pitch 72
Pratt and Whitney (engines) 101
Pre-take off checks 74
Prevailing winds 51
Public address systems 27

## Q

Qantas 110
QFE 76
QNH 76

## R

Radio beacons 60, 62, 76, 77
Refuelling 35, 38
    *see also* Fuel
Roll 72
Rolls-Royce (engines) 100, 101
Rio de Janeiro Galeao Airport 20
Rome Ciampino Airport 57
Rome Leonardo da Vinci Airport
    20
Runways 50, 78

## S

Safety regulations 90
Sharjah Airport 21
Simulators 86, 114
Singapore Airlines 20, 45, 113
Singapore Changi Airport 20, 42,
    43
Singapore Paya Lebar Airport 20
Skytrain 108
Smuggling 26
Stacking 55, 76
Stalling 95
Starting up 75

## T

Take off 42, 51, 74
Tokyo Narita Airport 10, 20, 50
Toronto Airport 20
Towing trucks 32
Tupolev TU-134 122
Tupolev TU-144 73, 122
Tupolev TU-154 123
Turbulence 75, 88, 94, 95
TWA (Trans World Airlines) 14,
    17

## V

$V_1$ (Velocity one) 75
$V_R$ (Velocity-rotate) 75
Vickers VC10 123
Vickers Viscount 123
VOR (VHF Omni-directional
    Range) 62, 64, 76

## W

Warning signals 82
Washington DC Dulles
    International Airport 16
Weather 74
Weather radar screen 88
Wide-bodied jets 108, 109

## Y

Yaw 72, 73

# Acknowledgements

The publishers would like to thank the following
organizations for their kind permission to reproduce the
photographs in this book:

Abex Jetway 30/31; Aer Lingus 117 (centre); Air Canada 17
(below), 64, 117 (below); Airbus Industrie 44/45, 116
(above); Alitalia 33 (above); Angus Fire Armour Limited 43
(above), 95 (above); Boeing Commercial Airplane Company
116 (below), 118 (above and centre); Braniff International
117 (above); British Aerospace 106/107, 119 (above);
Courtesy of British Airports Authority 1, 6/7, 27, 34/35,
42/43, 46/47, 54/55, 66/67, 76, 95 (below); British Airways
4/5, 23, 41, 63, 70/71, 80, 81, 83, 83 (inset below left),
86/87, 91, 92, 101, 102 (insets), 102/103, 111, 116 (centre),
118 (below), 120 (above), 123 (centre and below); Civil
Aviation Authority (UK) 94; Costain International Limited
10/11, 14, 56/57; Dallas/Fort Worth Airport 12/13;
Documentation Francaise, J. J. Moreau – Aeroport de Paris
16; EL AL Israel Airlines 36/37; Esso Petroleum Company
Limited 40; Flight International 119 (centre), 123 (above);
Gloster Saro Limited 43 (below); Courtesy of Sir William
Halcrow and Partners 15, 18/19, 51; Hong Kong
Government Office 50, 74/75; Houchin Limited 32 (above),
33 (below); KLM Royal Dutch Airlines 21, 119 (below), 121
(below); Lockheed-California Company 121 (above); LOT
Polish Airlines 120 (centre), 122 (centre); McDonell Douglas
Corporation 121 (centre), 122 (above); Novosti Press
Agency 122 (below); Fotokhronika Tass 120 (below);
Plessey Radar Limited 62, 68; Qantas Airways 90, 112,
113, 115; RFD Inflatables Limited 96 (both), 97; Smiths
Industries 83 (insets above left and below right); Spectrum
Colour Library 39; Trans World Airlines 17 (above); Zefa 2/3,
8/9, 32 (below), 37, 53, 58/59, 78/79, 88/89, 98/99.